"Real equity work is about identifying, responding and transforming structures, policies, procedures, behaviors, and biases that denied access and opportunities to underserved students. The authors of Equity Visits *provide a step in that direction. Having put 11 years of research and extensive fieldwork behind this project, the book provides a framework that spells out the specific steps in the process. It also provides protocols, samples, templates, and many other tools to facilitate its implementation."*

Waldo V. Alvarado
Director of Equity & Diversity
Reading School District, PA

"Educational leaders will benefit from a deep dive into equitable systems with a focus on instructional practice explored in this book. The authors provide a wealth of practical strategies and step-by-step processes to implement Equity Visits."

Eddie Ruiz
Assistant Superintendent Student Services, Equity & Access
School District of Palm Beach County, FL

*"*Equity Visits *documents the evolution of more than a decade of work among the New Jersey Network of Superintendents—from its focus on improvement of teaching and learning through instructional rounds, to visits with an explicit focus on improving equity practices. The book's many tools will enable educational leaders to collaboratively investigate schools and districts to understand the specific practices and cultures that perpetuate inequity. After reading this book educational leaders will better appreciate that change, especially focused on eliminating inequities, is slow and hard; develop effective strategies for talking openly about racial and other inequities; be equipped to process defeats on the way to success; and nurture leadership of all to sustain equity work."*

Dr. Linnea Weiland
Department Chair of Elementary and Early Childhood Education
William Paterson University, NJ

"The framework laid out in Equity Visits *provides an extension to learning walks and instructional rounds that will deepen outcomes for participants and their schools. The tools and ideas presented in this manuscript are practical and provide guidance that facilitators and district teams can utilize."*

Ellen S. Perconti
Superintendent
Grapeview School Districts, WA

"Equity Visits *is a long overdue addition to the literature regarding equity and inclusion. It tackles complex issues that underlie the persistent underachievement of marginalized students and provides a leadership framework that supports system improvements.*"

Maria G. Ott, PhD
Professor of Clinical Education
Rossier School of Education, University of Southern California, CA

"Equity Visits *provides an essential addition to the growing canon of literature about public education and diversity, equity, and inclusion. Chronicling over a decade of experiences of equity warrior teams, the authors capture the ups and downs of leaders who work across silos to brainstorm and try systemic solutions for the persistent structural and systemic diseases of racism, poverty, and kids left behind.*"

Perry Chen
Education Strategy Consultant
Oakland Unified School District, CA

"*Schools need tools to take a deep look at equity issues and take concrete actions. Leaders need guidance as well.* Equity Visits *takes a strong equity anti-racist focus and provides concrete strategies at the system level as well as instructional strategies, courageous leadership, and a process for gathering and analyzing important data.*"

Becki Cohn-Vargas, EdD
Educational Consultant, Coach, and Author
Cohn-Vargas Consulting

"Equity Visits *provides an innovative practice to support district and school leaders as they address inequities in the schools and in the classrooms. The inclusion of practical tools and resources that can be adapted by readers as they embark on and carry out their own work on the topic are especially useful for practitioners out in the field.*"

Carmella S. Franco, PhD
Author of *A Culturally Proficient Society Begins in School*

"*American education is at a crossroads. We must deliver on our obligation to educate all students at a high level or be prepared to put our country in decline. More children arrive at school burdened by poverty, by high rates of family mobility, as English language learners, or as members of other groups who have historically been underserved. We must make the choice to address the inequities that plague public education. This is a national imperative.*

"*The good news is that this challenge can be met. There are school leaders and school systems where that work is being done, where equity is being talked about and delivered. These accomplished authors have provided thoughtful analysis, tools, suggestions, and a vision of what can be. Please read the book carefully. It is up to you—to each of us—to address the educational needs of the most diverse student population in our history.*"

Jerry D. Weast
Founder and CEO
Partnership for Deliberate Excellence, LLC

"Today's public school system leaders are responsible for transforming teaching and learning through an equity lens. The complexity of this work requires theoretical frameworks, stories of success, and practical advice. The leaders and superintendents of the New Jersey Network of Superintendents have provided an invaluable resource for those who not only want to learn about equity, but want to act. By focusing on the power of equity visits, Roegman, Allen, Leverett, Thompson, and Hatch have given practitioners a set of tools and models that will enable them to start their own journeys of system transformation through an equity lens."

Joshua P. Starr, PhD
CEO
PDK International

"Whether we like to admit it or not, student achievement, college entrance rates, and so on are unequal among subgroups of students. Our society in general is not giving our students, or us as educators, good models of how to talk about and address the issues. Equity Visits *offers a structure to realize the inequities that happen, a protocol to start collaborating in finding solutions, and a method for starting to accept and discuss the issue to find solutions using a team approach."*

Leslie Standerfer
High School Principal
Estrella Foothills High School, AZ

"Building on the concept of instructional rounds and the work of courageous conversations, Equity Visits *is the perfect resource for schools and districts that are looking for ways to go deeper into race and equity in learning and keen to make an impact in their classrooms and schools."*

Sarah Zabel
Principal
Astor School, OR

"The work shared in Equity Visits *will help educators to be more purposeful in their work around providing equitable experiences for all students. The authors' approachable and informative writing style, their extensive research, and the inclusion of stories from fellow leaders make this work a more collaborative and reflective process. Doing equity visits will result in more positive outcomes in school improvements."*

Lena Marie Rockwood
Assistant Principal
Revere Public Schools, MA

Equity Visits

Equity Visits

A New Approach to Supporting Equity-Focused School and District Leadership

Rachel Roegman

David Allen

Larry Leverett

Scott Thompson

Thomas Hatch

Foreword by Edward Fergus

A JOINT PUBLICATION

A SAGE Publishing Company

FOR INFORMATION:

Corwin

A SAGE Company

2455 Teller Road

Thousand Oaks, California 91320

(800) 233-9936

www.corwin.com

SAGE Publications Ltd.

1 Oliver's Yard

55 City Road

London EC1Y 1SP

United Kingdom

SAGE Publications India Pvt. Ltd.

B 1/I 1 Mohan Cooperative Industrial Area

Mathura Road, New Delhi 110 044

India

SAGE Publications Asia-Pacific Pte. Ltd.

18 Cross Street #10-10/11/12

China Square Central

Singapore 048423

Acquisitions Editor: Dan Alpert

Content Development Editor: Lucas Schleicher

Senior Editorial Assistant: Mia Rodriguez

Production Editor: Jyothi Sriram

Copy Editor: Beth Ginter

Typesetter: C&M Digitals (P) Ltd.

Proofreader: Caryne Brown

Indexer: Robie Grant

Cover Designer: Candice Harman

Marketing Manager: Maura Sullivan

Printed in the United States of America

ISBN 9781544338132

This book is printed on acid-free paper.

SUSTAINABLE FORESTRY INITIATIVE

Certified Chain of Custody
Promoting Sustainable Forestry
www.sfiprogram.org
SFI-01268

SFI label applies to text stock

19 20 21 22 23 10 9 8 7 6 5 4 3 2 1

CONTENTS

Visit the companion website at
resources.corwin.com/equityvisits
for downloadable resources.

LIST OF FIGURES

CHAPTER 1

CHAPTER 2

CHAPTER 3

CHAPTER 4

FOREWORD
Equity as a Verb and a Journey

The work to address disparities involving race, ethnicity, language status, gender and gender expression, special education status, sexual orientation, and free/reduced lunch eligibility status is complex—not simply because of their long-standing presence but, most important, due to the interweaving histories of oppression that help to sustain these school-based disparities. Over the past two decades, conversations about these disparities have evolved as a result of substantive theories that outline some of the interwoven histories of oppressions; these theories have positioned the education field to finally do more robust exploration and repair. For instance, specific to race and ethnicity, Kendi (2016) outlines the manner in which racist ideas emerged from the early colonizers of the Americas to help justify their stealing of lands and people; Steele and Aronson (1995) note the manner in which these racist ideas are absorbed by racial/ethnic minority students as "floating signifiers"; Ladson-Billings (1995) describes the culturally responsive frames missing in the educational lived experiences of racial/ethnic minority children; Sue (2011) introduces the significance of language use that reifies racist sentiments; and many more. The work of addressing these disparities must now envelop these substantive theories into practices and activities for practitioners.

The 1947 case of *Mendez v. Westminster* was a watershed moment in which the U.S. Court of Appeals for the Ninth Circuit ruled that the segregation of Mexican American children in schools was a violation of the Fourteenth Amendment. This argument was followed by the 1954 case *Brown v. Board of Education* and this time ruled on by the Supreme Court. In both cases the argument was premised on the notion that segregation inherently shared the floating signifiers of racial inferiority and portrayed a racial hierarchy in our society. The notion of equity emerged as a substantive strategy for redressing a physical structure, such as school segregation; however, the strategy for undoing centuries of racial, ethnic, language, gender, and sexual orientation oppression hierarchies was still in development.

We are now poised with important theories to assist in undoing these hierarchies, and *Equity Visits* provides practitioners with yet another important tool that weaves together the elements of school structures that still require systematic dismantling as well as the mental models of equity leadership vitally important for sustaining this work. Each chapter provides substantive information from actual school districts that participated in the equity visits, and, most important, situates the wins and losses that can occur during a ten-year journey of developing and institutionalizing an equity lens. Practitioners utilizing this book should treat this book alongside others (e.g., Fergus, 2016; Hammond, 2017; Singleton, 2012) as necessary ingredients for a vitally important recipe. In addition, practitioners must consider this book as providing the verb-action embedded in the concept of equity as well as recognizing that achieving equity is not a one- to two-year endeavor. Instead, it is our part of the equity journey begun by many who have journeyed before through underground railroads, stonewalls, camps, and many more barriers.

—Edward Fergus

Author of *Solving Disproportionality and Achieving Equity: A Leader's Guide to Using Data to Change Hearts and Minds*

REFERENCES

Fergus, E. (2016). *Solving disproportionality and achieving equity: A leader's guide to using data to change hearts and minds.* Thousand Oaks, CA: Corwin.

Hammond, Z. (2015). *Culturally responsive teaching and the brain: Promoting authentic engagement and rigor among culturally and linguistically diverse students.* Thousand Oaks, CA: Corwin.

Kendi, I. X. (2016). *Stamped from the beginning: The definitive history of racist ideas in America.* New York, NY: Nation Books.

Ladson-Billings, G. (1994). *The dreamkeepers: Successful teachers of African American children.* San Francisco, CA: Jossey-Bas.

Singleton, G. E. (2015). *Courageous conversations about race: A field guide for achieving equity in schools.* Thousand Oaks, CA: Corwin.

Steele, C. M., & Aronson, J. (1995). Stereotype threat and the intellectual test performance of African Americans. *Journal of Personality and Social Psychology, 69*(5), 797–811.

Sue, D. W. (2015). *Race talk and the conspiracy of silence: Understanding and facilitating difficult dialogues on race.* Hoboken, NJ: John Wiley & Sons.

PREFACE

How long is 10 years?

In the career of a principal or superintendent, it might be the difference between beginning to understand the culture of a school or district and being able to influence beliefs and change practices.

In the life span of a network of educational leaders, it might be the difference between sharing success stories or bemoaning challenges and establishing the trust necessary to provide one another critical feedback on their work.

In the life of a child who has not experienced equitable opportunities, because of race or language or other differences, it is almost the entirety of their preK–12 school experiences—their best opportunity to gain the critical skills and knowledge they need to be prepared for college, the workforce, and democratic citizenship.

For the past 10 years, the authors of this book have served as facilitators and documenters for the New Jersey Network of Superintendents (NJNS). This network is a coalition of educational leaders dedicated to understanding how equity and instruction interact—and developing practices and policies that interrupt the myriad ways that these interactions harm students based on their race, gender, language, special education status, socioeconomic status, and other differences.

In this book, we share lessons we have learned about making equity central to the work of educational leadership. In particular, we focus on equity visits as a practice that supports leaders in investigating how inequities affect students' opportunities and outcomes in classrooms and schools. Along with equity-focused leaders from other schools and districts, superintendents and principals formulate strategies to challenge beliefs and change practices that sustain inequity.

We do not offer solutions to deeply engrained problems of inequity in this country. Instead, we seek to contribute to an expanding and deepening discussion about equity in schools and districts—to link arms with other educational leaders and organizations committed to creating more equitable schools for all children.

The focus of the network is New Jersey, a historically segregated state. New Jersey, however, represents a microcosm of the realities of schools and districts across the country. Just as we in NJNS have learned from equity-focused leaders from other states, we share lessons and resources from New Jersey with colleagues across the country.

While there are just five authors' names on the title page, equity visits were created by the superintendents who have committed their time and intellect to NJNS. Many speak directly in the text that follows, especially in the extended narrative reflections. Appendix A includes brief biographies of all of the participants in the network, as well as descriptions of their districts. This list illustrates the range of district types that have participated in the development of equity visits—rural, suburban, and urban.

We also acknowledge NJNS participants' leadership teams who have taken part in network meetings and equity visits, as well as the administrators, teachers, professional staff members, and students in the dozens of schools we have visited. We hope we have provided some useful feedback in return for the many valuable lessons we have learned from visiting them.

We recognize the leadership and dedication of our fellow founding design team colleagues, Robert Peterkin, Gail Davis and Ross Danis, as well as Edward Fergus, a stalwart critical friend. We are grateful for the support from the Panasonic Foundation, the Geraldine R. Dodge Foundation, and the Garden State Coalition of Schools.

We thank the Charles Dunn Hardie Trust Fund, College of Education, University of Illinois, Urbana-Champaign, for its support of the book, as well as Serena Salloum and Ruqayyah Perkins-Williams, for their feedback and assistance. We appreciate the support we have received from our editors at Corwin as well as the peer reviewers for the book.

David Allen thanks Fumio Someki for her unfailing patience and support. Larry Leverett acknowledges his wife, Debby, for the many years of support and encouragement provided over his long career as an equity warrior. Rachel Roegman thanks Joni Kolman, Tang Heng, Emilie Reagan, Sarah Woulfin, Robert Kliegman, and Sharon Kliegman for their support and encouragement—and especially, her wife, Sandi Roegman; Pups; and two children, Serena and Izzy, whose daily inquiries into what chapter she is on and where the pictures will go, have kept her on track.

ACKNOWLEDGMENTS

Corwin gratefully acknowledges the contributions of the following reviewers:

Waldo Alvarado
Director of Equity and Diversity
Reading School District
Reading, PA

Delores B. Lindsey
Educational Consultant, Co-Founder
Center for Culturally Proficient Educational Practice
Escondido, CA

Randall B. Lindsey
Educational Consultant, Co-Founder
Center for Culturally Proficient Educational Practice
Escondido, CA

Ellen S. Perconti
Superintendent
Grapeview School Districts
Grapeview, WA

Lena Marie Rockwood
Assistant Principal
Revere Public Schools
Revere, MA

ABOUT THE AUTHORS

Rachel Roegman is an Assistant Professor of Educational Leadership in the Department of Education Policy, Organization and Leadership at the University of Illinois, Urbana-Champaign. Her research examines the support and development of equity-focused leaders. Her work has been influenced by her experiences as a middle school teacher in traditional and alternative schools in the San Francisco Unified School District, and her commitment to anti-racist, equity-focused practice.

David Allen is an Associate Professor of English Education at the College of Staten Island, City University of New York (CUNY). His research focuses on how groups collaborate and create in schools and other settings. His most recent books include *Protocols in the Classroom: Tools to Help Students Read, Write, Think, & Collaborate* (with Tina Blythe, Alan Dichter, and Terra Lynch, Teachers College Press), *Facilitating for Learning: Tools for Teacher Groups of All Kinds* (with Tina Blythe, Teachers College Press) and *Powerful Teacher Learning: What the Theatre Arts Teach About Collaboration* (Rowman & Littlefield Education).

Larry Leverett is one of the co-founders of NJNS and the former Executive Director of the Panasonic Foundation, a corporate foundation with a mission of partnering with public school systems and their communities to break the links between race, poverty, and educational outcomes so that all students are improving academically and socially. Prior to that, he was a school superintendent in Greenwich, Connecticut; Plainfield, New Jersey; and Englewood, New Jersey.

Scott Thompson is one of the co-founders of NJNS and served as Assistant Executive Director of the Panasonic Foundation for 22 years. His publications include *Leading From the Eye of the Storm: Spirituality and Public School Improvement* (Roman & Littlefield Education) and numerous chapters, articles, and reviews. Prior to joining Panasonic Foundation, Thompson was Director of Dissemination and Project Development at the Institute for Responsive Education, where he edited the national journal, *New Schools, New Communities*, published in collaboration with Corwin.

Thomas Hatch is a Professor at Teachers College, Columbia University and Co-Director of the National Center for Restructuring Education, Schools, and Teaching (NCREST). He previously served as a Senior Scholar at the Carnegie Foundation for the Advancement of Teaching. He studies school reform efforts at the school, district, and national levels. His current work compares efforts to create more powerful learning experiences inside and outside of schools in "higher" and "lower-performing" education systems. His books include *Managing to Change: How Schools Can Survive (and Sometimes Thrive) in Turbulent Times* (Teachers College Press, 2009), and he is the founder of internationalednews.com.

NEEDED: EQUITY-FOCUSED LEADERS

We can, whenever and wherever we choose, successfully teach all children whose schooling is of interest to us. We already know more than we need to do that. Whether or not we do it must finally depend on how we feel about the fact that we haven't so far.

—Ron Edmonds, American Educator and Author

The United States is not fulfilling the promise of democracy in its schools. From pre-kindergarten through college, students' race, social class, and zip code continue to predict their educational experiences and outcomes. Beliefs about students' "deficits," or those of their families, are used to explain school systems' failure to accelerate the academic success of students of color, students living in poverty, students with disabilities, and students learning English as an additional language. In rural, urban, and suburban areas, school policies and practices, both formal and informal, are more likely to perpetuate inequitable systems than to challenge them. This results in students from underserved groups[1] having less qualified teachers, less rigorous curriculum, higher rates of suspension, and poorer performance on a range of academic outcomes.

These outcomes are not inevitable or irrevocable. Schools and districts across the country are making progress on increasing opportunity, access, and success for all students. While schools cannot solve societal poverty or racism, they can provide a high-quality education

---

[1]Throughout the book, we use the term *underserved* to refer to students of color, students living in poverty, students with disabilities, students learning English as an additional language, and students who experience various types of oppressions within schools and society. We chose this term because it connotes that institutions and the people who work within them are underserving students. Thus, people and institutions can change their practice so that all children are equitably served by preK–12 school systems.

for all children, including those historically underserved by preK–12 school systems—as a democracy demands.

This book introduces equity visits as an innovative practice that supports school- and district-level educational leaders in providing high-quality education for all students. In an equity visit, a school or district leadership team identifies a problem of practice defined by inequities in students' access to instructional opportunities and academic outcomes based on race, class, gender, disability, or language, or other characteristics. They bring leaders and other stakeholders into classrooms in one or more schools to observe instruction, interview teachers and students, and analyze other data related to the problem of practice. Collectively, the visitors and host team analyze these multiple sources of data to develop a set of patterns and wonderings to inform the host school or district about taking steps to remedy inequities. In the process, all participants deepen their knowledge of the different, often hidden, ways instruction and equity interact.

Several existing practices focus leaders on either equity (e.g., Childress, Doyle, & Thomas, 2009; Marshall & Oliva, 2006; Skrla, McKenzie, & Scheurich, 2009; Theoharis & Brooks, 2012) *or* instruction (e.g., City, Elmore, Fiarman, & Teitel, 2009; Downey, Steffy, English, Frase, & Poston, 2004; Fowler-Finn, 2013; Roberts, 2012). These practices address important aspects of educational leadership, but they often occur separately from one another. Equity visits, by design, investigate the convergence of equity and instruction. They do so by exposing leaders to the many ways that instructional practices, structures, and beliefs lead to inequitable educational experiences, in terms of both students' access to high-quality instruction and educational outcomes.

Equity-focused leaders recognize that inequities are sustained by beliefs and structures in their school's community and the larger society that are beyond their control. Equity visits represent their commitment to identifying problems of equity and take action in the ways and in the areas in which they *do* exercise influence.

LEADING FOR EQUITY IN A SEGREGATED STATE

New Jersey, where the work described in this book developed, offers a microcosm of the realities of societal inequities and their impact on preK–12 education. The state has the highest ratio of municipality to population, meaning that there are more towns, suburbs, and cities per person than any other state. Each municipality acts as its own school district. Because people are more likely to live in areas with people of similar racial backgrounds (Bonilla-Silva, 2017), this means that districts typically are segregated by race. In 2015, 20% of New Jersey towns were at least 90% white, though only 56% of the state population overall was white (O'Dea, 2016). The state's top five wealthiest municipalities were made up by at least 75% white residents (O'Dea, 2016). For the average Black resident in northern New Jersey, almost half of their neighbors were likely to be Black, even though only 11.8% of the state's population is Black (Fair Housing & Equity Assessment Report, 2015).

Students in New Jersey are more likely to attend segregated schools now than 25 years ago. The Civil Rights Project's most recent report on school racial makeup in New Jersey demonstrated that segregation in public schools is actually increasing: White and Asian families are more likely to reside in suburban and rural municipalities, while Black and Latinx families are more likely to live in urban areas (Orfield, Ee, & Coughlan, 2017). In the 1989–1990 school year, 22% of the 2,151 public schools in the state served a majority population of students of color. By 2015–2016, that percentage had more than doubled, with 46% of schools serving a majority population of students of color. Despite these patterns, there have been no recent efforts by the judicial or legislative branches to disrupt the patterns of segregation. A lawsuit by the New Jersey Coalition for Diverse and Inclusive Schools (2019) is underway at the time of this writing.

The stark residential segregation and associated educational inequities gave rise to the New Jersey Network of Superintendents (NJNS) and equity visits themselves. Throughout the book, we share firsthand accounts of superintendents, principals, and administrators from the districts who have participated in NJNS (see Appendix A). Their districts cut across the demographic categories that characterize New Jersey and the country: a few hundred students to almost 30,000; rural, suburban, and urban; majority white and majority minority; wealthy and poor. The lessons we have learned from the work of these leaders, who have committed themselves to challenge inequities within their schools and districts, extend beyond New Jersey into every state and community.

The responsibility for addressing inequity is every leader's work—no matter the demographics of their school or district. All districts face challenges of ensuring educational equity for all of their students, whether predominantly white or made up mostly of students of color. Educational leaders are responsible for ensuring that all students, regardless of who they are or where they live, receive the education that prepares them for college, career, and democratic citizenship.

Educational leaders cannot wait for courts or legislators to address structural and systemic inequities that lead to segregated schools. Rather, leaders must focus on addressing inequities within their buildings through equity-focused policies and practices.

DEFINING EQUITY-FOCUSED LEADERSHIP

Within their schools and district, educational leaders have the power to address structural and systemic inequities that impact students' day-to-day schooling experiences, opportunities, and outcomes. They create and implement formal and informal policies that assign students to different types of programs and coursework, including gifted and honors, special education, and second language acquisition (Loveless, 2011). They outline discipline policies, which may exclude students, especially Black and Latino males, from classroom learning through referral systems, suspensions, and expulsions (Smith & Harper, 2015). They could create policies that emphasize reconciliation and involve students in a system of restorative justice (Karp & Breslin, 2001). They influence staff hiring and assignment practices that often assign the newest teachers to their most difficult classrooms—or they work to ensure that high-need schools and classrooms are provided with principals and teachers equipped with the knowledge, skills, and dispositions to succeed (Cohen-Vogel & Osborne-Lampkin, 2007). Educational leaders, along with their leadership teams, adopt curricula and instructional approaches that may or may not provide relevance and rigor for all students.

Educational leaders develop, advocate, and implement policies and practices that directly impact the daily instructional experiences of students. Such choices are not neutral. All too often, as a result of school and district policy, Black and Latinx students and students in poverty are overrepresented in remedial courses and special education programs, and more likely to be disciplined, suspended, and expelled (Skiba et al., 2008). Conversely, these students are underrepresented in gifted and honors programs and coursework (Ford, 2011).

Equity-focused leaders, referred to by Larry Leverett (2011), one of the authors and founders of NJNS, as "equity warriors," are committed to the goal of achieving high levels of performance for all students, regardless of their race, class, or other demographic characteristic. "Equitable schools support students' development for full participation in society, family, community, and work settings; and they eliminate barriers to achieving equitable outcomes for all learners" (p. 6).

Pollack and Zirkel (2013) describe equity-focused leaders as individuals who advocate and implement "structural, pedagogical, curricular, or procedural change initiatives that are intended to correct identified disparities in educational opportunity or outcomes between groups of students" (p. 291). Equity-focused leaders strive to eliminate disparities by creating a shared vision of what equitable schooling looks like; framing shifting demographics as a benefit to their schools' diversity; working with teachers to develop new instructional approaches; engaging staff and community in long-term, systemic reform; and other ways. Leaders use data to identify and address disparities in access and outcomes, to analyze policies and practices that adversely impact different groups of students in different ways, and to better understand how school culture and environment create different learning experiences for students.

Robert Peterkin (2011), a founding member of the NJNS design team, argues that equity-focused leaders cannot simply be "raising the floor and lifting the ceiling." They cannot

be satisfied with simply providing the opportunity for all students to attend school, a goal that was part of the unfinished civil rights agenda of another era. The goal for them now, our goal for *this* era, is to improve student outcomes for those who were left behind *and* those who leapt ahead academically. (pp. 204–205)

DEVELOPING EQUITY-FOCUSED LEADERSHIP IN NEW JERSEY

As the former superintendent of Greenwich, Connecticut; Plainfield, New Jersey; and Englewood, New Jersey, Leverett knew firsthand the challenges of leading for equity in communities that were, for the most part, satisfied with how things were. He also knew at a deeply personal level the sense of isolation he experienced in this work. When he left the superintendency to serve as the executive director of the Panasonic Foundation, headquartered in New Jersey, Leverett brought with him the goal of creating a network to support like-minded superintendents in their development as equity-focused leaders.

Along with Assistant Executive Director Scott Thompson, Leverett created NJNS as a unique leadership development vehicle for New Jersey-based district leaders. In developing NJNS, Leverett and Thompson looked to existing networks of educational leaders as models. At the outset, they drew heavily on the work of the Connecticut Superintendents Network (CSN), led by Richard Elmore (2007), an organization that focuses on improving district leaders' instructional practice. They convened focus groups of practicing superintendents and consulted with the state superintendents' association and several New Jersey foundation leaders. They assembled a group of facilitators and documenters, which included former superintendents as well as university-based researchers, to serve as the design team for NJNS.

Finally, in December 2008, the New Jersey Network of Superintendents launched with 15 superintendents from urban, rural, and suburban districts across the state. In their first meetings, the founding members adopted the following theory of action:

IF NJNS engages New Jersey superintendents in a sustained effort to build a community of practice that

- focuses on the instructional core (the interrelationship of teacher and students around content);

- involves the disciplined use of instructional rounds in a variety of school settings; and

- provides learning experiences that address the adaptive and technical challenges of system-wide improvement efforts for ALL students in ALL classrooms,

THEN members of the NJNS Community of Practice will have demonstrably enhanced their own expert capabilities to observe and analyze the instructional core, and they will have increased their knowledge, skills, and dispositions to apply this learning to improving educational outcomes for ALL students in ALL classrooms in their school systems. ALL MEANS ALL.

The repeated capitalization of the word "ALL" was a deliberate reminder that school improvement must focus on all students. Educational leaders must not ignore pockets of low-performing students within high-performing districts. And they must not ignore patterns of disproportionality in students' instructional experiences, in terms of both access to high-quality instruction and academic outcomes.

Since then, NJNS has met monthly during the school year. Over 40 superintendents have participated from districts across the state. On any given year, the average number of superintendents has been 15. Some leaders joined NJNS as first-year superintendents, and one retired after 24 years as superintendent of the same district in her eighth year in NJNS. Two-thirds have been men and one-third women; two-thirds have been white, a quarter have been Black, along with three Latinx superintendents and one Asian superintendent.

The superintendents have led rural, urban, and suburban districts. Most have been traditional K–12 districts, but some have been high school only or K–8. One regional district provides alternative educational settings for court adjudicated and classified youth. Some districts have been majority minority, with over 90% Black and Latinx youth, most of whom qualify for free and reduced-price lunch. Other districts have consisted of almost equal percentages of racial groups (e.g., Black and white), and others are mostly white or white and Asian. Many have experienced changing student demographics as a result of shifts in immigration patterns and state and local housing policies. The influx of charter schools has also impacted some districts' enrollments, attracting higher-income white students.

At NJNS's monthly meetings, superintendents participate in a range of activities, all of which have evolved over time; these include the following:

- Developing individual and district theories of action for school improvement

- Analyzing district-level data to identify systemic inequities and developing strategies to address them

- Presenting equity goals and receiving critical feedback on these from peers

- Learning from experienced equity-focused leaders who are current or former district leaders

- Taking part in explicit discussions about race, and instruction, culture, and leadership

- Hosting and participating in instructional rounds and equity visits

While NJNS meetings initially included only superintendents and design team members, over time more and more meetings have involved members of superintendents' leadership teams. A recent equity visit included over 40 participants from 15 districts.

A core component of NJNS's activity, as noted in its initial theory of action, was using instructional rounds to develop shared understandings of effective teaching and learning. Instructional rounds, explained in detail in City and colleagues' (2009) *Instructional Rounds in Education*, is a school observation protocol aimed at developing participants' collective understanding of instructional practice. Instructional rounds within NJNS, which will be discussed in greater detail in Chapter 1, involved groups of superintendents and design team members visiting a number of different classrooms within a school, focused by a specific problem of practice identified by the host superintendent and principal. Each year, for the first several years of NJNS's history, three to five member superintendents hosted daylong instructional rounds within one of their district schools. In time, as we describe below, instructional rounds would evolve to become the equity visits that are at the heart of this book.

PUTTING EQUITY AND INSTRUCTION AT THE CENTER: EQUITY VISITS

Equity, as a term, is increasingly common in educational circles, though defined in many ways. Here is the definition of equity adopted by NJNS, the one we draw on in this book, and the one that applies to equity visits:

> Equity is achieved by raising the performance of all students and eliminating the predictability and disproportionality of student outcomes based on race, ethnicity, socioeconomic class, housing patterns, gender, home language, nation of origin, special needs, and other student characteristics. It requires the school system's provision of resources, supports, skills, and abilities essential to guarantee the preparation of all students for college without the need for remediation—ALL MEANS ALL.

This definition highlights the need to affect the *instructional core*, that is, the interactions of teachers, students, and curricular content (Cohen & Ball, 1999). It is not possible to achieve equitable experiences, opportunities, or outcomes without examining the interactions between teachers and students in relation to instructional content. Richard Elmore (2008) is clear about the centrality of the instructional core in student learning:

> There are only three ways to improve the quality of instruction and the quality of student learning: you can raise the level of the content, you can increase the knowledge and skill of the teacher, or you can change the role of the student in the instructional process. If you do any one of these things, then you have to do something about the other two pieces. (p. 43)

NJNS fuses its commitment to equity with a focus on the instructional core, integrating these within a professional learning community in which educational leaders identify key levers for change: school and district structures (e.g., policies, curriculum); culture and beliefs; and practices related to academic, discipline, and social-emotional outcomes. By focusing on instruction through an equity-focused lens, educational leaders bring sustained attention to developing and implementing strategies that address specific challenges in their schools and districts. These challenges include students' access to rigorous educational opportunities; disproportionality in disciplinary actions (e.g., suspensions by race, gender); and identification for and placement in special education. Inequities also manifest themselves in student outcomes related to achievement, graduation, and postsecondary pathways.

There are a range of ways leaders develop a dual focus on equity and instruction:

- Coaching and supervising administrators and teachers
- Aligning instructional initiatives designed to reverse long-standing trends pertaining to access, supports, and the success of students
- Developing policies that diminish or halt disproportionality in discipline actions
- Developing equitable decision-making processes for placement in special education and gifted programs
- Creating culturally responsive learning environments that embrace the diversity of student populations

NJNS's original theory of action, reproduced above, emphasized that close analysis of classroom practice would support superintendents' work as instructional leaders and lay the foundation for systemic, equity-focused change. Through this work, leaders would enhance the learning of all students, especially underserved students who are subject to inequitable systems and structures. In member districts, like those across the United States, this included students of color, students living in poverty, students with disabilities, and students learning English as an additional language.

But a focus on *all* students was not sufficient to challenge inequities for historically underserved students. Over NJNS's 10-plus years of practice, equity has moved from being an *implicit* rationale to an *explicit* focus of the work. This evolution, discussed in Chapter 1, illustrates how easy it is for equity to remain at the periphery of educational leaders' work, even when conducting instructional rounds and analyzing student achievement data. Chapter 1 describes how the NJNS design team, along with its members, recognized the need to make equity central to their practices. At the heart of this refocusing is the development of equity visits as a tool for leaders to examine issues of instruction and equity as a single problem, requiring a unified set of solutions.

The network began with one set of assumptions about equity and instruction, and in this book we share a different set of assumptions—namely, that equity must be named, placed at the center of data collection and analysis, and explicitly discussed at all levels of an organization. This latter set of assumptions guides the work of NJNS.

As we describe in the chapters to come, equity visits involve groups of educators conducting classroom observations and other data collection activities focused on an equity-related problem of practice. Our goal in describing equity visits and sharing tools from the visits and related practices is to support other educational leaders in identifying and addressing issues of educational equity in their own systems. For schools, districts, and networks that are already doing instructional rounds, this book can support educational leaders in making equity *and* instruction the focus for classroom observations. For leaders already engaged in equity initiatives, this book can support them in making stronger connections between those initiatives and classroom practice. For all leaders, the book provides resources for examining the intersections of equity and instruction. In every case, work on equity is a process without an end: The work of NJNS, and that of all of its participants, continues to evolve.

OVERVIEW OF THE BOOK

To support educational leaders in integrating their work on equity and instruction, each chapter focuses on a central question related to equity visits, equity, and instruction.

Why is it so hard to talk about equity <u>and</u> instruction? We begin Chapter 1 by considering why combining these two aspects of educational leaders' work is often difficult, even for those who are committed to being both instructional leaders and equity-focused leaders. We illustrate the need for explicit attention to equity with the story of how NJNS developed the practice of equity visits and describing the ways that NJNS participants worked to make equity explicit.

What is an equity visit? Chapter 2 provides a detailed explanation of equity visits organized by three key areas: (1) identifying an equity focus, (2) collecting and analyzing data through an equity lens, and (3) reflecting on the next steps of equity-focused work. The chapter includes specific examples of each element from an equity visit to Jersey City Public Schools, a racially, ethnically, and socioeconomically diverse district of almost 30,000 students, led by Superintendent Marcia Lyles.

What does an equity visit actually look like? Vignette 1 portrays an equity visit focused on mathematics performance. This vignette begins with the host principal determining the equity focus, describes some of the data collected by observers, and concludes with the principal's plan to move forward. We offer this story as an image of what one equity visit looks like, not as a model of what all should be. While based on an actual equity visit that took place within an NJNS member's district, due to the nature of the ongoing work in the district, names have been changed and some information has been modified to keep the district confidential (e.g., the percentages of students of different racial and ethnic groups have been changed).

How do educational leaders build a community that supports equity visits? In Chapter 3, we situate equity visits within the larger context of a school, district, or network. Educational leaders cannot conduct equity visits as stand-alone events—they need to be part of a larger and sustained strategy related to equity, instruction, and improvement. This kind of work supports leaders in initiating and sustained equity-focused changes. Work on equity is often resisted by some school staff and community members—and often isolating for individual leaders taking it on. In this chapter, we share some lessons we have learned about building an equity-focused community focused on three key features: relational trust, reflective practice, and professional accountability.

How can educational leaders respond to the challenges that arise in conversations about race? In Chapter 4, we focus explicitly on the need to address race in schooling and some of the challenges doing so entails. We consider how educational leaders' own racial backgrounds and experiences present both opportunities and challenges for leading conversations about race. We share four challenges that NJNS encountered when talking about race in education: the culture of nice, sticking to the protocol no matter what, understating race, and white silence. We include a series of anticipatory actions that can support leaders in having productive conversations about race.

What does talking about race productively look like? In Vignette 2, we provide an illustration of an extended, unplanned conversation about race that occurred at the end of an equity visit. This vignette shows how an equity-focused learning community can create space for individuals to share deeply held opinions, to learn from each other, and to reflect productively on issues of race and equity. As with the first vignette, identifying details have been omitted, but the dialogue is real.

What implications does our learning about equity visits have for the field? In Chapter 5, we conclude by considering implications from NJNS's learning for individual leaders, as well as broader implications for organizational culture, leadership preparation, and leadership professional development.

Appendix A provides a list of all of the superintendents who have been members of NJNS along with brief descriptions of their districts. This list illustrates the range of district types that have been affiliated with NJNS and the development of equity visits. Appendix B includes resources for readers who are interested in learning more about key ideas from the book, including conversations about race, instructional rounds, discussion protocols, equity-focused data analysis, descriptions of equity-focused leadership in action, and NJNS. Appendix C includes tools and resources for educational leaders who are interested in implementing equity visits. Appendix D includes the discussion protocols used in equity visits and other NJNS meetings. Corwin has also made the tools, resources, and protocols in Appendices B, C, and D available on resources.corwin.com/equityvisits.

Throughout the book, we bring in the voices of educational leaders who have been part of NJNS and its member districts. We include several extended excerpts from NJNS meetings or from our interviews with participants, highlighted as stand-alone text boxes. The leaders share how the practices we discuss have influenced their work as equity-focused leaders. Their voices represent just some of the school and district leaders with whom we have worked who are committed to addressing inequities in their systems. We share their voices to illustrate the real ways that they are taking up the call to create more equitable schools and districts for all of the students that they serve.

CHAPTER ONE

DEVELOPING EQUITY VISITS

We cannot seek achievement for ourselves and forget
about progress and prosperity for our community . . . our
ambitions must be broad enough to include the aspirations
and needs of others, for their sakes and for our own.

—César Chávez, American Labor Leader
and Civil Rights Activist

In this chapter, we first argue that school and district leaders need to address educational inequities in a sustained, focused, and explicit way. If they assume that this will happen without deliberately integrating their work on equity with their work on instruction, it is likely that systemic inequities will be ignored. To illustrate this, we share the story of how equity visits came to be—beginning with the initial instructional rounds practice of the New Jersey Network of Superintendents (NJNS). As we describe, even among educational leaders with a shared commitment to equity, NJNS members and the design team had to constantly change their practices to put equity at the center of the work. We conclude the chapter by highlighting lessons from that evolution that can support other leaders in the deliberate and explicit integration of work on equity and instruction.

In telling this story, we share both the successes and challenges NJNS faced in integrating the work of equity and instruction. The practice of equity visits evolved over time, and it continues to evolve as NJNS furthers its exploration of equity in diverse district contexts and as individual districts develop their own equity visit practices. Equity is not a goal to achieve but a constantly moving target as demographics, education policy and politics, and instructional practices shift. For this reason, equity visits as a leadership practice require continual reflection and refinement. Our story highlights how a group of superintendents and members of their leadership teams came together to identify and address systemic inequities within their state and district contexts.

MISSING: THE INTEGRATION
OF EQUITY *AND* INSTRUCTION

Observing classroom instruction and analyzing data for disparities are two common and important practices of educational leadership. In classroom observations, administrators and teachers regularly spend time observing teaching and learning as part of instructional rounds, classroom walk-throughs, teacher evaluations, and other initiatives. Often, classroom visits focus on a specific aspect of instruction, such as a dimension from a teacher evaluation framework, with the goal of building shared understandings of what this dimension looks like or should look like in practice. Visits may be used to ensure that teachers are implementing a particular curriculum or instructional strategy with fidelity. Following the observations, educators may share notes to determine if they had observed and assessed instructional practice in similar ways. Observers may also debrief the lesson with the teacher or analyze data collected across classrooms.

Another common practice is for schools and districts to disaggregate student performance data on statewide and school- or district-created assessments; sometimes this analysis includes other data sources such as discipline logs or attendance and graduation rates. In faculty meetings or professional development sessions, teachers and administrators examine data to identify patterns related to students' demographic characteristics (e.g., gender, race, or special education status), as well as patterns related to structural features, such as teacher assignments, grade level, subject area, and even specific standards. They look for inequitable student outcomes and consider the potential reasons for disparities in achievement.

These two school practices are both important: Educational leaders need both a solid understanding of effective teaching and learning and the ability to identify and address inequitable student opportunities and outcomes within their schools. However, these practices often are conducted in isolation from each other. Instead of pursuing instruction or equity on parallel tracks, what is needed is an approach that integrates them. As Theoharis and Brooks (2012) argue, "It is not enough to work to improve curriculum and instruction in a general sense; it is essential to increase access, processes, and outcomes through improved instruction" (p. 5). They go on to suggest that effective, equity-focused leaders must ground their work "in educational, indeed *instructional* access, process, and outcomes" (p. 6). Efforts to improve instruction almost never impact persistent systemic inequities without explicit and sustained attention to these. Despite the pressing need, there are few resources that focus attention on instruction and equity.

Even though widespread disparities in educational opportunities and outcomes are not new, educators often view equity as something in addition to the work—not the foundation of the work (García &

Guerra, 2004). As we illustrate in this chapter, equity can be an elusive target even among committed leaders who aim to make it the focus for their leadership practice.

The first part of the equation, leadership that focuses on improving instruction, is a well-established goal. Instructional leadership, a concept initially derived from the effective schools literature and focused on directive actions from the principal to the teachers, has expanded to include notions of transformational leadership (Hallinger, 2003). Hallinger (2003) described this evolution:

> As the top-down emphasis of American school reform gave way to the restructuring movement's attempts to professionalise schools in the early 1990s, transformational leadership overtook instructional leadership as the model of choice. As the 1990s progressed, a mixed mode of educational reform began to evolve, with a combination of top-down and bottom-up characteristics. (p. 342)

In this reconceptualized instructional leadership, also referred to as learner-centered leadership, administrators work with teachers to implement change, recognizing that one individual cannot create the types of change needed to ensure success for all students. Practices such as instructional rounds (City, Elmore, Fiarman, & Teitel, 2009; Hatch, Hill, & Roegman, 2016; Roegman, Hatch, Hill, & Kniewel, 2015) offer one way to support the development of a shared understanding of teaching and learning.

In instructional rounds, administrators and teachers observe classrooms, paying close attention to the teaching, learning, and curricular content evident there. These observations, typically organized around a problem of practice related to instruction, are meant to develop participants' understating of instruction and student learning and develop a common language for discussing and improving teaching and learning. Along with teacher evaluations, professional development, and curriculum development, instructional rounds engage leaders in discussions about instruction and student learning.

The second part of the equation, equity, is less well developed. Even in the context of developing instructional leadership, equity and related concepts such as social justice, diversity, and multiculturalism are rarely addressed. Theories of leadership, such as transformative leadership (Shields, 2010), that call on leaders to consider systemic inequities and act on them, are often discussed separately from theories that focus specifically on instruction. When leadership preparation programs or professional development sessions address issues of equity, they often do so in seminars, courses, or readings that stand apart from the day-to-day life of the school. For example, many leadership preparation programs include a single course on multiculturalism or social justice.

In other words, equity is not explicitly connected to the work related to instruction (Marshall, 2004; Roegman, Allen, & Hatch, 2017). Parker and Villalpando (2007) demonstrate that educational policies for curriculum or instruction are more likely to perpetuate existing inequalities in students' opportunities and outcomes than to address them. To truly address inequity, educational leaders need an explicit and sustained approach that makes equity explicit.

SHIFTING FROM INSTRUCTION TO EQUITY *AND* INSTRUCTION

NJNS's development of equity visits illustrates how committed equity-focused leaders developed an explicit focus on equity within their work on understanding and improving instruction. NJNS began with a strong commitment to address systemic inequities, made explicit in its theory of action that "ALL MEANS ALL." However, its early practice demonstrates how focusing on instruction can leave out paying attention to equity.

The key shifts we describe below were made possible by regular cycles of reflection on the part of NJNS's design team and the network as a whole. Our reflections drew on Argyris's (1977) concept of "double-loop learning," an approach to organizational learning that requires practitioners to think critically about why initiatives succeed or fail and to question underlying assumptions. As part of NJNS's practice as a learning community, design team and superintendent members regularly reflect on our learning about systems-level leadership related to equity, instruction, and progress related to our theory of action and norms (discussed in Chapter 3). As the story of the evolution of rounds into equity visits illustrates, this continual reflection allowed us to identify a set of essential ingredients to integrate equity with our work on instruction:

1. Explicit, clearly articulated expectations for naming existing inequities in access and outcomes

2. Disaggregated data, beyond year-end test scores, to understand the "hows" and "whys" of existing inequities in instructional practice

3. Opportunities to reflect on and refine the work happening within schools

4. Shared understanding of key terms and concepts, including instructional equity and equity-focused leadership

These "essentials" underlie NJNS's evolution over time as equity-focused leaders worked to create school and district cultures that integrate equity and instruction.

Addressing the Challenges of Keeping Equity at the Center: Creating Equity Visits

We describe NJNS's shift to the use of equity visits in three "eras." Throughout the three eras, NJNS regularly visited schools in participating superintendents' districts and observed a range of problems of practice related to instruction and equity. While the design team and participating superintendents were deeply committed to equity in education, our ongoing reflection on NJNS's activities made it clear that the practice of instructional rounds was not supporting the types of conversations needed for instructional improvement for all students, particularly students of color and other underserved students. These reflections prompted the changes from one era to the next. For each era, Figure 1.1 highlights changes in the focus of the visits, the types of data collected, and learning objectives for the participants.

Figure 1.1 NJNS Eras Examining Equity and Instruction			
	Era 1: Instructional Rounds	**Era 2: Issues of Equity**	**Era 3: Equity Visits**
	Years 1 and 2	**Years 3 through 5**	**Years 6 through 11**
Focus of Problem of Practice (POP)	Instruction	Instruction connected to district-identified issue of equity	Equity goal connected to instruction
Data Sources	Observations in several classrooms in one school	Observations in several classrooms in one school	Observations in one or more schools; interviews with staff and students; reviews of student work
Targeted skills and outcomes	• Building capacity for nonjudgmental description of teaching and learning, and for identifying patterns in evidence observed • Building shared understandings of teaching and learning	• Identifying inequities within one's system • Deepening understanding of how systemic inequities play out in classroom practice	• Developing specific goals to address identified inequities • Deepening understanding of how systemic inequities play out in classroom practice

Era 1: Instructional Rounds

NJNS's initial approach to rounds followed the example of the Connecticut Superintendents' Network (CSN), facilitated by Richard Elmore and Lee Teitel (City et al., 2009; Elmore, 2007). In our first daylong meetings, we focused on developing participants' skills as non-judgemental observers of instruction, and on developing a common understanding of teaching and learning. Each rounds visit was hosted by a superintendent who selected a school within their district to be the focus. The host, along with various members of their leadership team, developed a problem of practice for the visit, an issue or challenge directly related to instruction. (See Chapter 2 for a more detailed explanation of terms such as problems of practice, look-fors, patterns, and wonderings.) Before entering the classrooms to observe, the host shared a brief presentation about the problem of practice, as well as relevant data, such as demographics and test scores. The host outlined a series of "look-fors"—specific elements of instruction related to the problem that guide the observation, such as "What evidence of students posing questions do you observe?" and "Are learning objectives visible in the classroom?" Then, for about two hours, in small groups, super-intendents and design team members visited four to six classrooms for about 10–15 minutes each. In each classroom, they recorded observations related to the problem of practice and look-fors. Figure 1.2 presents an example of a problem of practice and set of look-fors from a rounds visit from Era 1; together, they highlight that era's emphasis on instructional practice.

Figure 1.2   Sample Problem of Practice and Look-Fors from a Visit in Era 1 to Grover Middle School in West Windsor-Plainsboro Regional School District

We want teachers to incorporate self-awareness language and patterns into daily teaching practices, to provide a variety of learning experience and assignment choices that mirror student learning patterns, and to allow students to reflect on their learning patterns before beginning assignments so they can develop learning strategies.

Is there evidence of students using self-assessment strategy cards?	Are learning patterns evident in student agendas?	Are there word walls with self-assessment language?	Are teachers referring to learning patterns during lessons or in assignments?	Are students talking about their learning patterns?

After the classroom observations, the small groups reviewed their notes and identified patterns across classrooms related to the problem of practice. They also framed a small number of "wonderings," also related to problems of practice, for the host team to think about. Each small group presented its patterns and wonderings to the whole group, as well as any district and school representatives invited by the host superintendent. Next, either in small groups or as a whole, superintendents developed and presented a series of recommendations for the host school. The day concluded with NJNS members reflecting on their learning about the instruction.

Over our first two years of instructional rounds practice, NJNS focused on developing superintendents' abilities to be descriptive and nonjudgmental in their observations. This was meant to support leaders in understanding and discussing the complexities of instructional practice rather than simply or immediately evaluating it, a typical expectation for administrators. Samuel Stewart, retired county superintendent of Mercer County, shared a reflection during a rounds visit in Era 1 that was typical of the era: "It is the focus of rounds that makes it so powerful. I think it is taking one of key ideas of the instructional core, teacher, student, and content, and focusing on that." In reflecting on the first years of NJNS, design team members and superintendents felt, like Stewart, that they were improving individually and collectively in their ability to observe and discuss classroom practice. At the end of the second year, Jacqueline Young, then superintendent of the Essex Regional Services Commission and since, retired, commented:

> . . . this past year [with] rounds, I was really pleased. We made good progress in terms of improving over the previous year . . . in terms of being able to be descriptive, in terms of us being more focused on what we actually see instead of what we think we should see.

When the design team met following a rounds visit in the spring of the second year, members recognized that important things had been missing from the whole-group conversation: The focus on instruction, while necessary, had pushed the equally important focus on equity to the side. One design team member, Robert Peterkin, described observing a classroom for students with disabilities: It was populated entirely by Black and Latinx boys. "When," he wondered, "would we talk about that type of observation?" While equity was central to NJNS's mission, it had remained implicit in NJNS's work.

As the design team reflected on NJNS's first two years, it recognized that classroom observations during rounds visits had raised concerns related to equity, such as the observation shared about the predominance of boys of color in a self-contained class. However, when these concerns were raised during a whole-group conversation, most participants felt that, while the pattern might be real, it was not their responsibility to address it if it was not directly connected to the host's stated problem of practice. They may also have hesitated to name inequities for fear of appearing too critical of their colleague's school—reflecting what City and colleagues (2009) call the culture of nice, which they maintain is pervasive in education. (We discuss the culture of nice in greater detail in Chapter 4 and present some suggestions for ways to support educational leaders in giving and receiving critical feedback.)

Reflecting on school visits, meeting agendas, and participant reflections over the summer at the end of NJNS's second year, design team members and superintendents realized an explicit attention to equity was necessary to support members in connecting equity and instruction. NJNS needed to modify its practices so that equity moved from the periphery to the center.

Era 2: Issues of Equity

At the final meeting of Year 2 and at the start of the following year, NJNS explicitly began to modify its practices to highlight intersections of instruction and equity, within rounds visits and other network activities. NJNS initiated this refocusing in the final meeting of Year 2 with guest speakers Jerry Weast and Frieda Lacey, then superintendent and deputy superintendent of Montgomery County Public Schools, Maryland. Weast and Lacey shared one key strategy from their district's work that involved mapping the district demographics. They identified "green zone" schools, which were situated in the more affluent and white areas of the county, and "red zone" schools, in which there were higher concentrations of children of color, children in poverty, children learning English as an additional language, and children requiring special education services (Childress, Doyle, & Thomas, 2009). In response to the mapping, schools in the red zone received a greater share of district resources, such as smaller class sizes and additional reading coaches.

NJNS participants commended Weast and Lacey's approach to equity and instruction in Montgomery County. Several NJNS members visited Montgomery County the following year to learn more about the work, and some adopted specific strategies used in that district, such as analyzing data from the National Student Clearinghouse Research Center to track graduates' college pathways or developing a set of benchmarks along the preK–12 continuum to ensure students are on track for college completion. Over the summer, all members received a copy of the book *Leading for Equity* (Childress et al., 2009), which described Weast and Lacey's work in Montgomery County. These measures signaled a shift in NJNS focus.

The opening meeting of Year 3 was designed to focus attention on issues of equity through Weast and Lacey's red and green zone approach. Each superintendent was asked to identify a red zone related to inequity of some kind in their own district and develop a systemic strategy to address it. While red and green zones referred to geographic areas in Montgomery County, in many cases, NJNS superintendents used the term to identify disparities in student access or outcomes that were connected to student characteristics, such as disability status, racial or ethnic group, or performance on standardized assessments. A district might identify students receiving special education services, for example, as its red zone, instead of a school or set of schools in a specific neighborhood. Hosts of rounds visits were expected to use their identified red zone in framing the problem of practice for the visit.

Superintendent Margaret Hayes of Scotch Plains-Fanwood Public Schools was one of the first to host a visit in Era 2. At the time, her suburban district was 76% white, 11% Black, about 6% Latinx, and 7% Asian. For her red zone, she identified specific demographic groups of students who were underperforming on state assessments. These included Black and Latinx students and students with disabilities. The problem of practice Superintendent Hayes developed, illustrated in Figure 1.3, demonstrates the more explicit focus on equity in this era. At the same time, the look-fors demonstrated the continued focus on instructional practice related to literacy and engagement.

Superintendent Hayes's problem of practice recognized two demographic groups of students that were not performing at the same level as other groups. The problem asked observers to examine the types of learning opportunities students have in different classes. Observers

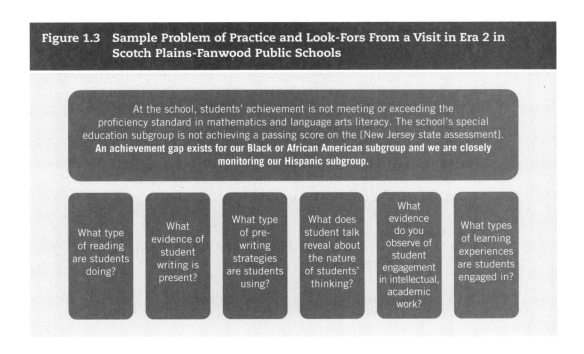

Figure 1.3 Sample Problem of Practice and Look-Fors From a Visit in Era 2 in Scotch Plains-Fanwood Public Schools

At the school, students' achievement is not meeting or exceeding the proficiency standard in mathematics and language arts literacy. The school's special education subgroup is not achieving a passing score on the [New Jersey state assessment]. **An achievement gap exists for our Black or African American subgroup and we are closely monitoring our Hispanic subgroup.**

| What type of reading are students doing? | What evidence of student writing is present? | What type of pre-writing strategies are students using? | What does student talk reveal about the nature of students' thinking? | What evidence do you observe of student engagement in intellectual, academic work? | What types of learning experiences are students engaged in? |

were directed to pay particular attention to the instructional tasks in which students of color were engaged. In analyzing and reporting out from the classroom observations, issues of race came up more frequently than they had in instructional rounds visits from Era 1. For example, NJNS members began to note the racial composition of different classrooms, even if that was not a specific look-for. They also noted students' racial backgrounds in considering which students were called on by teachers.

The use of the term red zone receded as NJNS moved into Year 4. This was due primarily to the absence of identifiable geographic zones in a number of districts, and also to new members' lack of familiarity with Weast and Lacey's work in Montgomery County. However, the increased emphasis on equity remained. All superintendents were asked to identify issues of equity within their districts. For some districts, the identified inequities related to students' race and socioeconomic status. In high-performing and predominately white suburban areas, many superintendents identified disparities in opportunities and outcomes for students receiving special education services.

For the three years that made up Era 2, half of the rounds visits focused on an issue of equity. Examples include a visit focused on the performance of students with disabilities in general education classrooms and one focused on the level of rigor in different tracks of language arts (remedial, general, and honors). While this represented an increase from Era 1, the fact that not all of the visits focused on equity demonstrated the continuing struggle to put equity at the center.

At the end of a rounds visit in Year 5, the final year of Era 2, one superintendent wrote an anonymous reflection on the impact of the focus on equity during instructional rounds:

> *The intersections between having students participate in 21st century skills and achieve high levels of cognitive engagement presents challenges when we simultaneously focus on "all means all." What scaffolds will this type of cognitive engagement require as students enter school with different backgrounds, both cultural and in prior preparation?*

The superintendent's closing question reflects NJNS's increased attention to the different, and often inequitable, experiences of students from diverse backgrounds within the same classrooms and school.

NJNS reflections on rounds visits shifted from a focus on the instructional practices identified in the host problem of practice, as was typical in Era 1, to looking for evidence of how district inequities were made apparent in classroom practice. It was now common for superintendents to consider how issues of equity observed in the host school might relate to their own district and what actions districts could undertake to support the learning of all students.

PARTICIPANT REFLECTION

Sharing the Pit-of-the-Stomach Feeling About Systemic Inequities

Superintendent Hayes reflected on a rounds visit to a neighboring district that focused on observing different programs aimed at supporting students who receive special education services. The observers had shared concerns about the low level of academic rigor in self-contained classrooms and raised this as an area for the hosts to consider. Her reflection illustrates how the visit helped her think both about the special education services observed as well as the challenges she faced in her district (see Figure 1.2 earlier in this chapter). Superintendent Hayes began her reflection by speaking to the host and then shifted to her own work:

> You [the host school] have to calibrate where you see you are in the process, recognizing that all schools are struggling with trying to bridge the gap, particularly between special education and general education students. If anyone of us knew exactly how to do that, we would have done it a long time ago.
>
> We're all dealing with this challenge. When the network came to my district, we were in the same place relative to focusing on special education. I shared the pit-of-the-stomach feeling because I walked out after that visit with this question of rigor. One concern we have is the Common Core State Standards are high, and some kids are [not able to meet them currently]. How do we fill in the gaps while raising them up to meet the standards? That is the challenge we all face.

Era 3: Equity Visits

The increase in attention to equity in Era 2 rounds visits was commented on by design team members and superintendents alike. However, the design team and many superintendents felt that NJNS was only sporadically touching on the topic of racial equity. They also noted that only half of the visits in the previous years had addressed any component of equity, meaning that half did not. Furthermore, as demonstrated by Superintendent Hayes's problem of practice from Era 2 discussed earlier in this chapter, several visits included a problem of practice that was focused on equity while the look-fors focused on students generally rather than focusing on the specific inequities identified in the problem of practice.

Following a summer planning retreat for Year 6, involving several superintendents and all design team members, NJNS introduced an alternative structure for visiting schools. The new structure, called equity visits, was meant to increase the explicit attention to issues of equity, particularly racial inequities in student access and achievement, during the visits. The equity visit protocol would require that the problem of practice include a clear connection to equity. (See Chapter 2 for a detailed description of the equity visit protocol.)

In the first meeting of Era 3, the design team, after consultation with superintendents involved in the summer retreat, shared its perspectives on these shifts as it introduced the program plan for the year with the following call to action:

> We know that opportunities to learn are not equitably distributed to all students. Efforts to provide more equitable opportunities are needed at all levels of the school system, from the boardroom to the classroom. NJNS, over the past several years, has evolved into a community that is anchored in a commitment to educational equity. The superintendents represent diverse school districts: rich and poor, urban and suburban, high performing and low performing. Equity challenges in the districts are as diverse as the districts themselves, and districts must tailor solutions that reach into classrooms in ways that are keenly responsive to their student populations.

The team introduced the expectations, crafted with representative superintendents at the retreat, for the new equity visits, including the clear connection to equity in the problem of practice and look-fors. To deepen their examination of existing inequities, data collection expanded to include interviews with teachers, students, and possibly other stakeholders. The design team began asking hosts to provide disaggregated data from state assessments and internal assessments related to the identified problem of practice.

Superintendents expressed their readiness to take on the challenges associated with a clearer focus on equity. As a result, through Era 3, all equity visits have explicitly addressed existing inequities in at least some aspects of the visit, such as the problem of practice or look-fors, or in the ways that host superintendents introduced the visit, such as providing disaggregated data or district racial context.

Figure 1.3 illustrates a sample problem of practice and set of look-fors from a visit early in Era 3 to the Freehold Regional High School District, a district of high schools serving eight diverse K–8 school districts. The equity visit focused on a long-standing concern on the part of district leaders about the equitable opportunities, access, and performance of students with disabilities. Participants observed classrooms with a co-teaching model. Co-teaching, new to the district, involved pairing one general education teacher and one special education teacher in teaching a shared group of students. In addition to observations, participants interviewed teachers who taught in co-teaching classrooms to learn about their perspectives on this instructional model. Combining classroom observations and teacher interviews provided participants with a range of perspectives on the co-teaching initiative and how well it was supporting students.

Do we have effective practices to support equity of access to learning goals and increased achievement for every student? Are our co-teaching classes (heterogenous classes with one special education-certified teacher and one content area-certifed teacher) effective?

| What types of co-teaching models are teachers using? | How are both teachers differentiating instruction for indivdiuals or small groups? | What does it mean to effectively co-instruct in co-teaching classroom? | [To what extent do] both teachers have an established role and contribute to instruction, management, assessment, and planning? | [To what extent do] students respect each teacher's role in the classroom? |

PARTICIPANT REFLECTION

Dismantling Systemic Barriers Across Demographic Difference

An early equity visit in Era 3 took place at Sojourn High School, a school located with a juvenile detention center, which is part of the Essex Regional Education Services Commission. Almost all of the students at Sojourn are Black and Latino males and qualify for free or reduced-price lunch. Superintendent Charles Sampson, whose problem of practice and look-fors were shared in Figure 1.3, reflected on the visit to Sojourn—so different from his own district student population, which is over 75% white and has fewer than 10% of students who are economically disadvantaged. Despite the differences in demographics, Superintendent Sampson connected issues of barriers and access across district contexts:

> I spoke with a group of incarcerated youth, all young African American males, about their aspirations for life after incarceration. After each young man articulated a clear goal of graduating high school as a means of getting off the streets, I inquired about how long they had been incarcerated.
>
> Their responses shocked me as many had been jailed for periods exceeding 14–15 months while awaiting trial. The systemic barriers to their reaching the goal of graduating high school were severe. Yet each young man clearly recognized the benefits of a high school diploma. I could not reconcile their hope with the reality of the system that had locked them up for such large portions of their young lives while awaiting trial.

(Continued)

(Continued)

Their reality helped me to further commit myself to the paradoxes of my own system where we had implemented large-scale changes to provide access, opportunity, and support to students in an effort to create more equitable outcomes for all. Like those young men, our aspirations did not represent our reality. While our [district] numbers soared, we had students who were not soaring like others. That moment at Essex Regional helped to question my own district successes in a harsher manner. The hope expressed within a system designed to deny opportunity further strengthened my resolve to continue to dismantle the barriers in my own system while encouraging me to not hesitate to begin to question others who were not dismantling their own systemic barriers wherever they might be found.

LEARNING LESSONS ACROSS THE ERAS

The changes described above that marked the evolution from rounds to equity visits took place over six years and affected a range of NJNS practices. The shift was possible because the design team members and superintendents continually assessed their practice in an ongoing, reflective manner. Summer retreats, in particular, provided time for design team and representative superintendent members to step back from the pressing aspects of planning a visit and working together as a learning community to reflect more deeply.

Following Year 9, as the product of one such summer retreat, NJNS embarked on Year 10 with a theory of action that differs in significant ways from the initial one we shared in the Introduction.

IF superintendents work together in an **equity**-driven learning community in which they are supported and challenged to do the following:

- Focus on ensuring rigorous intellectual engagement for **all students**, with **special responsibility for students who have been historically underserved**

- Identify and pursue **systemic equity goals** in their districts

- Examine and discuss the **role of race and other aspects of difference** in their work

- Develop their understanding of how to engage colleagues, board members, and community in their work on **equity and race**

- Review data on their **equity goals**, reflect on their progress, and share what they are learning both inside and outside NJNS

THEN we, as individuals and as a network, can be more effective in **eliminating disparities in access, support, and academic and social outcomes** for all students.

We put in boldface the words and terms that reveal the explicit attention to race and equity in the revised theory of action. This theory of action clearly integrates equity and instruction. It calls out race and historically underserved students, and it acknowledges disparities in access, support, and outcomes. It is this theory of action, with its explicit attention to equity, race, and disparities in students' outcomes, that serves as the foundation for equity visits.

HOST REFLECTION

Learning to Throw Stones at Goliath

Jeffrey Moore, superintendent of Hunterdon Regional High School District and former director of curriculum for the Freehold Regional High School District, also a member district, reflects on how hosting an equity visit in his former district supported him in integrating his work on equity and instruction:

[At Freehold] We were in the home stretch of hosting our own equity visit—an examination of access, opportunity, and inclusion practices for students receiving special education services. Prior to the visit, we had spent weeks crunching data on our problem of practice. We had made logistical arrangements for classroom visits in several schools. It had been a large program to arrange. Unfortunately, as we prepared for the equity visit, some of us drifted into the same frame of mind that we occupy for other types of accountability-driven tours, like state monitoring and accreditation visits. I found myself in danger of treating the equity visit like something to complete, something that would not live past the moment of saying our goodbyes and the visitors pulling out of our parking lot. It began to feel like something separate from my daily work.

Then, the day arrived. We took tours of classrooms. We discussed our data with visitors. In the closing events of the day, we received feedback in the form of questions from our visitors and then sat in a fishbowl as a district team to openly reflect on that feedback. The questions were challenging, in that they had pulled at deep roots of our practice—deeper than anything we had anticipated. I felt overwhelmed and dizzy from the feedback. We had somewhat approached the equity visit as putting on a show, but the visitors had dug out our assumptions about special education and inclusion, and they laid them bare, belly-up.

I heard myself saying: "There's too much to do." And I heard Larry Leverett [a design team member] say: "Jeff, when you do equity work, there's always too much to do."

(Continued)

> *It was a crystallizing moment for me, one to which I often return to remind myself of my place in the work, the humility that the work demands, and the rejuvenating and clarifying power of relationships with those who are doing the same work. The work is always bigger than each of us, but that is no license to stand down. In a practical sense, the moment melded what had been two separate conversations in my leadership brain: one conversation about continuous improvement, and one about equity. On a much different level, it taught me something about what it means to throw stones at Goliath.*

Equity visits have surfaced important questions about the integration of equity and instruction and their relation to leadership practice:

- Is improving instruction in general enough to achieve equitable outcomes? Or do schools need to target different instructional approaches for different groups of students?

- What does equitable instruction look like in a classroom? How can equitable instruction be rigorous for all students? How can equitable instruction be observed?

- Should problems of practice focus on the experiences of all students, or should they focus on the specific groups of students experiencing inequitable opportunities and/or outcomes within a school or district?

- To what extent should educators examine beliefs, values, and assumptions about race in relation to instruction and academic success? What impact does *not* doing so have on progress toward equitable experiences and outcomes?

These are not questions that lend themselves to easy or quick answers. Nor are they the only questions for educational leaders to take up. But the conversations within NJNS and within districts that take up questions like these illustrate how equity visits can support educational leaders to address inequities of race, class, and disability, among other systemic inequities within preK–12 schools and systems. Linking conversations about equity to conversations about instruction positions educational leaders to develop and enact strategies for improvement that have the potential to positively impact academic opportunities, experiences, and outcomes for all students, especially those who have been underserved by their schools and districts.

While we cannot offer answers to the critical questions that have emerged in equity visits, we can share several lessons we have learned about supporting educational leaders in integrating working on equity and on improving instruction. While related to observing classroom instruction, these lessons reinforce the necessity of putting equity at the center of all work on instruction:

- Educational leaders are more likely to create equity-focused problems of practice when they have explicit, clearly articulated expectations to name the specific inequities that they aim to address.

- The inclusion of multiple data sources is essential to informing a deep and nuanced understanding of how equity and instruction interact within a school or district context.

- In addition to school visits, educational leaders need time and structures to reflect on their learning related to equity and instruction; to increase their knowledge and skills related to specific aspects of equity and instruction; and to build a trusting learning community with colleagues where risk taking is valued.

- Educators must develop shared understandings of what equity is and how inequities are manifested in classroom practice, school structures, and district organization.

These lessons are contextualized in the coming chapters of the book. For example, in Chapter 2, we describe how equity visits incorporate a range of sources of evidence in addition to classroom observations, including interviews with students and teachers, data on course-taking patterns, reviews of student work samples, and others. In Chapter 3, we examine the role of learning communities rooted in relational trust, reflective practice, and professional accountability.

As we share these lessons with others beginning or already engaged in the work of integrating equity and instruction, we recognize that our own work is evolving. Each equity visit affords the opportunity to try out lessons from reflecting on previous visits, as well as to examine particular problems of practice related to equity and instruction framed by the host. The practice of equity visits, like the work on equity itself in schools, districts, and society, is always a work in progress.

CHAPTER TWO

A DETAILED LOOK AT EQUITY VISITS

*You don't make progress by standing on the sidelines,
whimpering and complaining. You make progress by
implementing ideas.*

—Shirley Chisholm,
First African American
Congresswoman and
First African American
Female Presidential Candidate

In most cases, when principals or superintendents (the host) invite educators from outside the school or district into their classrooms and schools, they are likely either being evaluated formally or celebrating academic successes. In an equity visit, however, the host invites observers to investigate a systemic inequity in students' educational experiences, opportunities, and outcomes. Instead of accolades or a formal evaluation score, the host expects to receive feedback related to the inequity under investigation and support in moving forward in addressing it.

Equity visits serve two key purposes: (1) supporting the host leadership team in deepening its understanding of the identified inequity in order to effectively address it, and (2) developing the observers' understanding of equity and instruction in order to support their own equity-focused practice. While the host and members of the leadership team will receive specific feedback to inform action steps and further inquiry, both hosts and observers will deepen their understanding of the interaction of equity and instruction.

Equity visits may be conducted as part of a district's professional practice, in which each school takes a turn hosting—what we refer to as an in-district visit. They may also be conducted as part of professional learning community or network with members from different districts—a cross-district visit. For in-district visits, the principal is typically the host, and observers are typically principals and assistant principals from other schools, as well as central office administrators such as directors or supervisors. Teachers from the host school may also participate in the visit. In cross-district equity visits, such as those in NJNS, the superintendent is typically the host, and observers are superintendents from other districts and members of their administrative teams, including assistant superintendents, curriculum supervisors, and principals.

In both cases, the visit is planned by a host leadership team that includes the superintendent or principal and other educators who plan and carry out the work associated with the visit and related activities. An equity visit itself is typically a one-day event. In the morning, observers collect evidence related to an equity focus. They might observe classrooms; interview teachers, students, and others; review disaggregated data; or examine student work samples. In the afternoon, they analyze the evidence from these activities and develop and present a set of patterns and wonderings to the host team for reflection and action.

CORE ELEMENTS OF AN EQUITY VISIT

While the visit takes place on just one day, it actually represents a process that begins well in advance of the visit and continues long afterward. In this chapter, we describe three elements essential to planning, conducting, and learning from equity visits: (1) identifying an equity focus, (2) collecting and analyzing data through an equity lens, and (3) reflecting on and planning next steps of equity-focused work. Figure 2.1 illustrates the sequence of core elements that a host team follows in planning and conducting an equity visit. In order to illustrate each element, we share examples from an NJNS equity visit to Jersey City Public Schools, a racially, ethnically, and socioeconomically diverse district of almost 30,000 students led by Superintendent Marcia Lyles.

The elements we describe and illustrate in this chapter are meant to provide a framework for educational leaders engaged in equity work, not a model to be followed lockstep. Each district, school, or network will adapt the framework and the tools included for its own context and equity focus. The goal is to use these elements to foster conversations among educators about equity and instruction, conversations that advance the work on increasing equitable instruction, policies, practices, and outcomes for underserved students within the school or district being visited.

Step 1: Identifying an Equity Focus

At the cross-district level, as in NJNS, equity visits are initiated when a participating superintendent volunteers to host a visit at a school or schools within a district. At the in-district level, equity visits may be introduced by the superintendent as part of a strategic plan

Figure 2.1 Equity Visit Core Elements

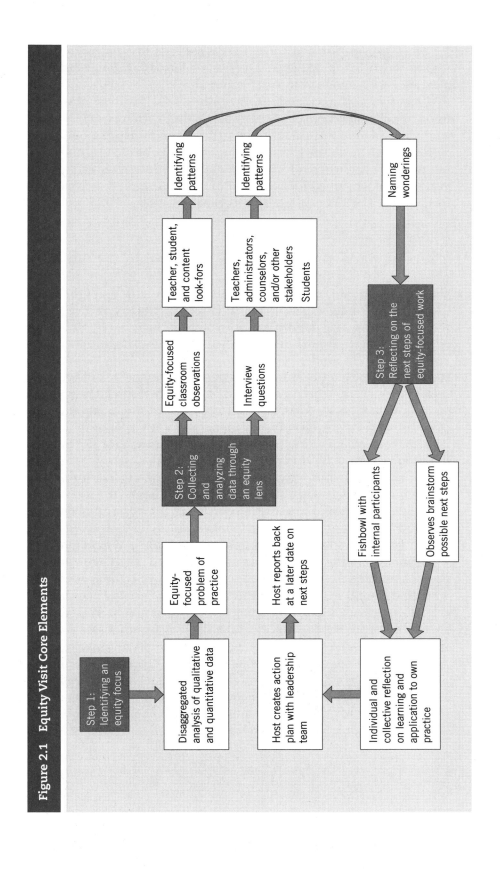

for all schools to work to address issues of inequity; for example, in Hillsborough Township School District and Jersey City Public Schools, all schools host equity visits on a rotating basis.[1]

Whether hosting a cross-district or in-district visit, the host relies upon a leadership team of experienced administrators and teacher leaders to plan and conduct the visits, as well as use the outcomes from visits (patterns, wonderings, and reflections) to identify and carry out next steps. The team follow three important steps to plan for the visit: naming an equity focus, determining the scope for the visit, and formulating a problem of practice to guide the visit.

Naming the Equity Focus

The leadership team's first step in planning an equity visit is to identify the equity focus. The equity focus refers to the issue that the visit will investigate. For example, an equity focus might highlight racial disparities in students' placement in gifted classrooms or investigate the rigorous learning opportunities for students learning English as an additional language and how that relates to their standardized assessment scores. The leadership team begins by examining data related to student outcomes or access in order to identify areas of inequity related to instruction. Data may include conventional school- and district-level data, such as standardized assessments, discipline referrals, or course enrollment. Host team members may also analyze additional data sources such as climate surveys, parent surveys, or notes from informal classroom observations.

Whatever the data sets, they should be disaggregated by relevant demographic groups (e.g., race, poverty status, language proficiency, disability, or gender). Through these analyses, the host team begins to articulate an equity focus. The focus may be related to an existing strategic goal (which may or may not already be explicit about equity) or highlight a new or overlooked area of work (e.g., related to curriculum, professional development, or school or course selection processes). The goal should be framed in language that is concisely communicable to all stakeholders and participants in the visit, observers as well as school staff members. (In Appendix B, we share resources that can support schools and districts in using data to identify an equity focus.)

In developing an equity focus for Jersey City Public Schools, Superintendent Marcia Lyles and her leadership team analyzed disaggregated data from district benchmark assessments, attendance records, and state assessments, amongst another data sources. The district has a population that is 38% Latinx, 32% Black, 16% Asian, and

---

[1]Within Jersey City Public Schools, these visits are called rounds; for clarity in this chapter, we use the term equity visits to highlight the expectation that all principals focus explicitly on equity as they develop their problems of practice and plan the visits.

10% white; 68% of students are economically disadvantaged. Through their analysis, they found that Black and Latinx students consistently had less access to intellectually rigorous coursework, such as Advanced Placement (AP) courses. These students were also more likely to experience poorer academic outcomes in terms of retention, graduation, and achievement on state assessments.

The leadership team developed specific targets and timelines for the district to address these inequities. For example, they set goals that by the end of Year 1, there would be increased participation of Black and Latinx students in Algebra I. By the end of Year 3, there would be increased participation in AP courses and increased graduation rates for Black and Latinx students. In developing the in-district equity visit schedule, Superintendent Lyles directed principals to focus equity visits on these district goals.

As in Jersey City, naming an equity focus invariably involves educational leaders and other stakeholders talking explicitly about race, class, gender, special education status, and other topics that are not always easy for educators to discuss. They need to identify and name the groups of students in their schools or districts whose educational experiences and outcomes are inequitable. Chapter 4 focuses specifically on the challenges of talking about race in the United States; several of the key challenges and suggestions are applicable to other cultural and demographic groups that are also underserved or marginalized, including LGBTQ students, students learning English as an additional language, and homeless students.

The process of developing an equity focus is not always neat or linear. Different types of data afford different perspectives on equity and instruction within a school. An initial focus may be identified but then modified or rejected as new data are considered. This iterative process is actually beneficial for host leadership team members. Superintendent Patrick Michel of Salem City School District reflected on the process of developing an equity focus as a team, which he found to be as valuable a learning opportunity as the visit itself:

> *Getting ready for the equity visit in and of itself is professional development. It makes you take a hard look at your equity goals. When [the network design team] sent something back asking, "What do you mean by this? Why are you using that piece of data?"—addressing those questions is professional development unto itself. A lot of conversations happen within the school leadership team before the observers come in, conversations that may happen anyway. But I don't think they happen as intentionally.*

Determining the Scope for the Visit

After naming an equity focus, the host team determines the scope for the visit. Since an equity visit can address only a small slice of a school's work, it is crucial to consider which part of that work will be the most productive for investigating the equity focus. For example, an equity visit that is focused on inequities in upper elementary grade students' opportunities to develop literacy skills might best be examined through visits to K–3 classrooms as well as literacy-intensive fourth and fifth grade classrooms; for a visit that is focused on reading at the secondary level, observers might visit classrooms in multiple subject areas in order to investigate literacy across the curriculum.

Typically, there are more classrooms within the scope than the observers can realistically visit, so a sampling strategy is required. For example, hosts may choose to visit classrooms of both newer and more veteran teachers; or they may recruit two classes from salient grade levels and/or categories (e.g., resource, mainstream, and inclusive classrooms). When the team makes such decisions with principals, assistant principals, curriculum supervisors, and teachers, these key stakeholders will learn more about the purposes for the visit (i.e., inquiry rather than evaluation) and are more likely to buy into the visit. In general, it is best to avoid mandating that any individual teacher's classroom be visited.

For Superintendent Lyles and her leadership team in Jersey City, the equity focus on Black and Latinx students led them to target four of their six high schools that were identified by the state as low performing or in need of improvement. Students assigned to these schools, mostly Black and Latinx, were less likely to complete Algebra 1 by the end of ninth grade, less likely to be promoted to tenth grade, and less likely to graduate from high school in four years. Their educational experiences were markedly different from those of students assigned to the district's other high schools. The district had redesigned the ninth-grade year in an attempt to increase students' performance and engagement. For the NJNS equity visit, the host team chose to have observers visit freshman classes in the Freshman Academies at these four schools.

Formulating the Problem of Practice

In addition to determining the scope for a visit, the equity focus supports the host leadership team in framing a problem of practice for the visit. The problem is the central question or issue that observers focus on in collecting and analyzing data during the visit. A "rich problem of practice," according to City, Elmore, Fiarman, and Teitel (2009),

> focuses on the instructional core; is directly observable;
> is actionable (is within the school's or district's control and
> can be improved in real time); connects to a broader strategy
> of improvement (school, system); is high-leverage (if acted
> on, it would make a significant difference for student
> learning). (p. 102)

In addition to meeting these criteria, equity visit problems of practice name specific groups or categories of students experiencing inequitable educations—those identified in developing the equity focus.

In preparation for an equity visit from NJNS to the four high schools, Superintendent Lyles and her leadership team in Jersey City developed a problem of practice based on the equity focus related to Black and Latinx students' participation and completion of more rigorous coursework:

> *How do we implement, with fidelity, innovative, research-based strategies that support high intellectual performance opportunities and personalize learning to meet the diverse strengths and interests of all students?*
>
> *The Freshman Academy is a research-based model designed to help students successfully transition to high school through a nurturing, personalized environment that will support a more challenging instructional program to prepare students for college and career. We have the structure. Now we must get to the core.*

This problem of practice models the criteria introduced above. It focuses on the *instructional core* by drawing attention to a range of student performance opportunities that can be observed in classrooms. The problem is connected to the district's *strategic plan* to have all students engage in more rigorous academic work. It is *actionable*, addressing structures and pedagogies within teachers', principals', and the district's control. It is also *high-leverage*—developing opportunities for intellectual work has the potential to make a significant difference for student learning outcomes.

In terms of the crucial additional criterion for an equity visit, this problem of practice focuses on those students attending Freshman Academies, a structure put in place at the four targeted schools to support Black and Latinx students in successfully completing ninth grade. While the problem of practice does not specifically name Black and Latinx students, in the NJNS meeting prior to the visit and in the opening presentation the morning of the visit, Superintendent Lyles made clear to observers that racial disparities in various student outcomes were the driver for the equity visit.

Step 2: Collecting and Analyzing Evidence through an Equity Lens

After the host leadership team identifies an equity focus, determines the scope for a visit, and develops a problem of practice, it identifies the forms of evidence observers will collect and analyze. These will include evidence from two primary sources: classroom observations and interviews with stakeholders. Stakeholders may include students, teachers, administrators, guidance counselors, or others whose work connects to the problem of practice. Parents and community members, often overlooked in educational leadership practice (Ishimaru, 2013), can also serve as interviewees. Additional forms of evidence that may be collected include student achievement data, discipline referral data, climate surveys, and student work samples. Some of these data sets may have been used by the host leadership team in developing the equity focus; now they will be reviewed by an external group of experienced leaders.

As observers prepare to collect evidence, they are divided into small groups of four to six participants. Each group has an assigned facilitator/time. Much of the day is spent in these small groups, with the whole group coming together at the end of the day to share out the patterns and wonderings developed based on the evidence they collected. Figure 2.2 illustrates the schedule for the equity visit to Jersey City, breaking down how much time was spent on different parts of the day. Note that these times are a suggestion, not a requirement. (See Appendix C for a template for creating an equity visit schedule.)

Figure 2.2 Sample Equity Visit Agenda (Jersey City Public Schools)

Time	Minutes	Activity
8:00–8:20	20	Breakfast and welcome at the District Office
8:20–9:00	40	Setting the stage—overview of the district's and each school's equity focus and problem of practice (superintendent and principals)
9:00–9:25	25	Divide into 8 groups and travel to the four schools (two teams per school)
9:30–11:00	90	Classroom visits (four classrooms per group)
11:00–11:30	30	Interviews of students and/or teachers (three to five interviewees in each)
11:30–12:30	60	Small group deliberations [see Appendix D: Developing Patterns and Wonderings Protocol]
12:30–1:00	30	Travel back to District Office
1:00–1:45	45	Lunch
1:45–2:45	60	Small groups report out patterns and wonderings to whole group
2:45–3:15	30	Host superintendent and principals reflect on what they heard and their initial thinking about next steps [see Appendix D: Fishbowl Protocol]
3:15–3:30	15	Observer reflections on the day (written and discussed)

In this section we look first at two key tools in collecting and analyzing data related to the problem of practice and equity focus: classroom observation look-fors and interview protocols. In relation to these, we describe some of the challenges of keeping equity central to data collection.

Look-Fors. Classrooms are—or should be—busy, dynamic environments, with lots going on at any given moment. Look-fors identify a small set of *specific* foci for observers to pay close attention to. Look-fors are often framed as questions, such as "What questions does the teacher ask?" or "How are students interacting with each other?" In framing these, it is useful to allow for more open-ended look-fors such as these that require observers to take detailed, descriptive notes, rather than yes/no ones, such as "Are students interacting with each other?" Collecting evidence of look-fors is different from collecting evidence for other observation purposes, such as a formal teacher observation. As a result, clarifying for observers the purpose for look-fors and the types of evidence to be collected will be critical to everyone contributing to and learning from the visit.

Because problems of practice are grounded in the instructional core, look-fors typically focus observers on seeing what students are saying or doing in the classroom, what teachers are saying or doing, and the task(s), standards, and content students are working on. In NJNS, it has been helpful to develop two to four look-fors for each category: teacher, student, and content. This leads to an average of about nine or ten look-fors in total. Figure 2.3 illustrates the look-fors for the equity visit to Jersey City.

Each observer takes only one of the three categories and focuses on the subset of look-fors for just that category. (See Appendix C for a template that can be used to assign roles for small groups.) If a small group has six members, each category may be assigned two observers. Having each observer focus on only one category is helpful as look-fors involve extensive note-taking, such as recording what the teacher says and does, asking several individual students about how they understand the purpose of a task they are working on, or compiling notes on curriculum materials posted in the room. In Figure 2.4, we share an excerpt from notes taken by one observer (in the teacher observer role) in two different classes during this visit. (In Appendix C, we include a template that a host can modify to support observers in taking notes related to evidence of look-fors.)

Interview Protocols. During an equity visit, each small group of observers typically interviews groups of teachers, students, or other members of the school community. These conversations are brief, 20 to 30 minutes at most. Having a protocol—a list of questions to

Figure 2.3 Sample Look-Fors (Jersey City Public Schools)

What evidence is there that the <u>teacher</u>:
- Poses questions that require students to explain their thinking and/or reasoning?
- Provides support for struggling learners through individualized instruction or peer-to-peer assistance?
- Provides opportunities for student discussion and/or collaboration centered on the objective?

What evidence is there that the <u>students</u>:
- Integrate technology to deepen their understanding and/or find unique approaches to problem solving?
- Provide evidence-based reasoning to support responses?
- Can articulate what they are learning and why (it is important)?

What evidence is there that the <u>content or task</u>:
- Is reflected in posted student work where teachers provide meaningful feedback that redirects and pushes students to the next level?
- Is a catalyst for deeper thinking and problem solving?
- Provides opportunities for students to engage in discussions/activities that extend their learning and relate to the stated objective?

Figure 2.4 Sample Note-Taking Sheets From Two Classrooms (Jersey City Public Schools)

Subject Matter: Algebra 1   **Grade Level:** 9th and 10th   **Time:** 9:55–10:05

What evidence is there that the **teacher**:	
• Poses questions that require students to explain their thinking and/or reasoning?	T asks, "Who has the answer to number five?"
	T says, "Good job. Now who has the answer to number six?"
	T says, "No, x does not equal 17. Can someone help him out?"
• Provides support for struggling learners through individualized instruction or peer-to-peer assistance?	T says, "Okay, everyone look back at number six and solve it at your table."
	T walks around and looks at students' work at the two tables in the back of the room. T does not say anything.
• Provides opportunities for student discussion and/or collaboration centered on the objective?	T says, "J, can you come to the board and show us how you solved the problem?"

Subject Matter: Geometry   **Grade Level:** 10th   **Time:** 10:15–10:25

What evidence is there that the **teacher**:	
• Poses questions that require students to explain their thinking and/or reasoning?	T asks, "How did you determine the area of the polygon?"
	T asks, "Did anyone try a different strategy?"
	T calls on three students to come to the board and write down their strategies.
• Provides support for struggling learners through individualized instruction or peer-to-peer assistance?	T asks, "What do you notice about the different strategies?"
	T asks, "Why did they all get different answers?"
• Provides opportunities for student discussion and/or collaboration centered on the objective?	T asks, "What is a strategy you could use to check your work? At your table, discuss how you could check your work on this problem and come up with one strategy."

be asked—keeps interviews focused on the problem of practice. The protocol also supports each team in collecting comparable evidence from the multiple interviews going on during a visit. Talking with teachers or students in a group (e.g., three interviewees) makes those being interviewed more comfortable than feeling they are facing a panel of four to six interviewers; it also allows for interaction among the individuals being interviewed.

Just as with choosing classrooms to observe, the host leadership team considers which interviewees could best shed light on the problem of practice and equity focus. For example, if the problem relates to how special education-certified teachers and content area-certified teachers are implementing a co-teaching initiative, it is important to ensure teachers from both certification areas are interviewed. If the problem focuses on different educational experiences of Black and white students, the host team ensures that both Black and white students are interviewed.

For the equity visit to the Jersey City high schools, with its problem related to intellectual performance opportunities and personalized learning, the host team developed interview protocols for the teachers (four questions) and students (five questions) (see Figure 2.5). For the teachers, the protocol focused on the interviewees' perspectives on student engagement, collaboration, and professional development. For the students, the protocol asked interviewees to comment on which of their classes challenged them, how they collaborated with classmates, and how they were supported by teachers in preparing for college and careers.

Possibilities for data collection are myriad. An equity visit in Neptune Township School District focused on a problem of practice around college attendance, stating "students do not get equal levels of parental and organizational support regarding course selection, pathways, [or] secondary options." To investigate this problem, Superintendent Tami Crader and her leadership team invited guidance counselors, as well as students, to participate in interviews. After the visit, Department Chair of Guidance, Juan Omar Beltran, reflected that interviewing students and guidance counselors was invaluable. He found that "the interviews provided a road map for where some deficiencies in equity exist, and possible solutions to those concerns." Other potential stakeholders for equity visits, depending on the equity focus and problem of practice, include families, paraprofessionals, student services staff, classified staff, and community members.

Ensuring that each observer group has the chance to observe in multiple classrooms and conduct one or more interview sessions makes scheduling a visit challenging. Figure 2.6 provides a sample schedule.

Making Equity Explicit in Data Collection. Keeping equity at the center of a visit's data collection is challenging. While the equity focus is clearly named by the host leadership team in framing the visit and in

Figure 2.5 Sample Interview Questions (Jersey City Public Schools)

Teacher Interview Questions

1. How familiar are you with the school's instructional priorities or Problem of Practice?
2. What does "student engagement" look like in your classroom?
3. What structures are in place for you to collaborate with your colleagues?
4. What type of professional development have you been provided, and what would you like to see?

Student Interview Questions

1. Which classes challenge you to think and problem-solve?
2. How often do you have the opportunity to work collaboratively with your peers?
3. What supports are in place if you or fellow students need additional help?
4. What do your teachers and school do to prepare you for college and careers?
5. What more do you believe you need to be prepared for success?

Figure 2.6 Sample Data Collection Schedule

Time	Group A	Group B	Group C
9:25–9:35	Classroom Visit to Ms. A, Room 124	Classroom Visit to Mr. C, Room 114	Classroom Visit to Ms. B, Room 137
9:40–9:50	Classroom Visit to Ms. B, Room 137	Classroom Visit to Ms. A, Room 124	Classroom Visit to Mr. C, Room 114
9:55–10:05	Classroom Visit to Mr. C, Room 114	Classroom Visit to Ms. B, Room 137	Interviews with teachers, library
10:15–10:25	Classroom Visit to Mr. D, Room 121	Interviews with students, guidance office	
10:35–10:45	Classroom Visit to Mr. E, Room 132		Classroom Visit to Ms. A, Room 124
10:50–11:00	Interviews with students, guidance office	Interviews with teachers, library	Classroom Visit to Mr. D, Room 121
11:05–11:15			Classroom Visit to Mr. E, Room 132
11:20–11:30	Interviews with teachers, library	Classroom Visit to Mr. D, Room 121	Interviews with students, guidance office
11:35–11:45		Classroom Visit to Mr. E, Room 132	

creating the problem of practice, the equity focus will look differently in the look-fors and interview protocols, as well as other data collection activities. For example, if a problem focuses on teacher expectations for Black and Latinx students, one of the teacher look-fors might ask observers to tally how often teachers call on students of color versus white students, and to take notes on the nature of those interactions (e.g., length of interaction, follow-up questions, type of questions). In an interview, observers might ask students of all racial backgrounds—Black, Latinx, Asian, white, multiracial, Native American—how their teachers challenge them academically.

One challenge in focusing on race and other student demographic characteristics is that it is not possible to be certain of a student's racial or ethnic identity just by looking at them, nor is it possible to know if a student is receiving special education services, is economically disadvantaged, or identifies as LGBTQ; even gender cannot be assumed. Nevertheless, it is critical that participants in equity visits strive to identify how different groups of students experience their schools and classroom differently—even if this means sometimes making an incorrect assumption about a student's demographic characteristics. It helps to keep in mind that the purpose of the data collection is to identify patterns, not come to definitive conclusions—and never to make evaluations of or recommendations for individual students or teachers.

Another challenge comes with including named inequities in a problem of practice and set of look-fors. When they are not named explicitly, it is less likely for inequities, and particularly, racial inequities, to be discussed. But naming them may be difficult in terms of district culture or politics, especially in communities where naming race has historically been taboo. At other times, the named inequities may be a central but implicit aspect of the problem, such as in the Jersey City visit used as an example in this chapter. There, the look-fors did not identify race as an area of concern, nor did the interview questions probe students or teachers to discuss race. However, over 90% of the students in the Freshman Academies at all four schools are Black or Latinx; in contrast, at the district's highest performing high school, about 35% of the students are Black or Latinx. Thus, it was clear to Superintendent Lyles and her team that visiting these four schools was a deliberate choice to focus on the experiences of Black and Latinx students—and they made this clear to observers in the presentation at the beginning of the visit.

In Figure 2.7, we offer some possible look-fors and interview questions that illustrate ways to explicitly collect data related to identified inequities. We use the term "students of color" in the explicit equity focus look-fors purposefully here, knowing that someone might appear one way but identify themselves a different way. Another risk exists in paying specific attention to any one group of students: This may lead observers to not pay attention to other groups. We acknowledge this possibility; however, we

Figure 2.7 Sample Equity-Focused Look-Fors and Interview Questions

General Focus	Explicit Equity Focus
Classroom Observation	
What evidence is there that the teacher poses questions that require <u>students</u> to explain their thinking and/or reasoning?	What evidence is there that the teacher poses questions of <u>students of color</u> that require them to explain their thinking?
What evidence is there that the teacher provides opportunities for <u>student</u> discussion and/or collaboration around on the lesson objective?	What evidence is there that the teacher structures activities so that <u>linguistically diverse students</u> collaborate or engage in discussion about content?
What evidence is there that the <u>students</u> provide evidence-based reasoning to support responses?	What evidence is there that <u>Black</u> students provide evidence-based reasoning to support responses?
What evidence is there that the <u>students</u> can articulate what they are learning and why it is important?	What evidence is there that the <u>students receiving special education services</u> can articulate what they are learning and why it is important?
What evidence is there that the content or task is reflected in <u>posted student work</u> in which teachers provide meaningful feedback that redirects and pushes students to the next level?	What evidence is there that the content or task is reflected in posted student work in which teachers provide meaningful feedback to <u>all work samples</u>?
Interview Protocols	
Teacher: How familiar are you with the school's instructional priorities or Problem of Practice?	Teacher: How familiar are you with the district's Problem of Practice related to <u>Black and Latinx student outcomes</u>?
Teacher: What does "<u>student engagement</u>" look like in your classroom?	Teacher: What does "student engagement" look like for <u>students from different racial backgrounds</u> in your classroom?
Student: Which classes challenge <u>you</u> to think and problem solve?	Student: Are <u>all students</u> equally challenged in their classes?
Student: What do your teachers and school do to prepare <u>you</u> for college and careers?	Student: Do your teachers think <u>all of your classmates</u> can go to college? How does a student's <u>race</u> influence teachers' expectations of them?

argue that when a host has analyzed data and identified an equity focus, it is important that this specific group of students remain central to the data collection. As new concerns arise, including those related to other groups, host teams may shift, expand, or rethink their equity focus. This is consistent with our understanding of equity-focused leadership as a sustained process of ongoing reflection, analysis, and action.

Analyzing Evidence

Classroom observations, interviews with students and teachers, and other activities that a host team has planned provide the observer groups an array of evidence with which to work. In the following sections, we describe the stages that small groups and the full group go through to analyze the evidence and formulate possible patterns and wonderings related to the problem of practice and equity focus.

Identifying Patterns. After the small groups have completed their evidence-collection activities—usually followed by a lunch break—they reconvene to analyze the evidence and develop a set of patterns and wonderings. First, group members review their individual note-taking sheets from observations, interviews, and other evidence-collection activities to refamiliarize themselves with the evidence and identify possible emerging patterns related to the problem of practice. Then, collectively, the group works to identify possible patterns. Some groups proceed from role to role, e.g., beginning with evidence related to student look-fors, then moving on to teacher look-fors, and so on; others construct patterns and wonderings by moving chronologically through the evidence collected, classroom by classroom, interview by interview, and so on. Patterns are often directly related to the look-fors, e.g., identifying the extent or frequency of teachers posing a certain type of question or the different ways students expressed being supported by their teachers. (See Appendix D: Developing Patterns and Wonderings Protocol.)

However patterns are identified, they must be supported by evidence. If only one observer identifies a particular pattern (e.g., teachers are less likely to call on students of color), the small group deliberates, with each member sharing evidence so that they agree that the pattern is well-supported rather than a possible "one-off." Patterns may be derived solely from observations or interviews, or from a combination of both, as well as any other data collection (e.g., review of student work samples or climate survey data). Drawing on multiple data sources to develop a pattern is more likely to occur when there is a deliberate overlap between the look-fors and interview protocols, or other evidence-collection activities. For example, if the problem of practice focuses on engagement and gender, observers in the classroom might look for ways that male, female, and non-binary students engage in class activities; and interview questions might ask for students' perspectives on their engagement, with observers paying attention to whether students of different genders respond in similar ways, or not.

While groups work toward consensus for each pattern they present, at times, this will not always be possible. In such a case, a group may choose to present a "minority opinion" pattern, letting the full group know that, based on the evidence they collected, they could not come to agreement but felt it was important to present. Such cases often give rise to productive wonderings, as we describe below.

After conducting classroom observations and interviews during the equity visit to Jersey City high schools, one small group developed the following patterns:

- In one of five classrooms, teachers posed questions that required students to explain their thinking.

- In five out of five classrooms, students had opportunities to discuss content.

- There was little evidence of specific supports for struggling learners or differentiation.

- There was evidence of student engagement in their coursework.

The first two patterns were derived solely from observations, while the final two were based on both interviews and observations.

At times, a pattern emerges that does not relate directly to a look-for or interview question, but does relate to the problem of practice and/or equity focus. For example, a team might have observed evidence of students of color raising hands and not being called on in a whole-class discussion; even if not related to one of its look-fors or if it did not happen in every classroom, it is critical to call out this evidence.

In reporting out patterns derived from interviews or classroom observations, groups strive to avoid making it likely that host administrators can identify any individuals who took part in the interviews or taught a specific class. This is not easy to do, given that the teachers, students, and others participating in interviews will be assigned by name to meet with specific groups, often on a printed schedule; thus, it may be possible for host personnel to identify specific individuals. The same is true for the schedule of classroom observations.

One way to avoid the risk of identifying individuals is to report patterns based on interviews and observations combined. Another strategy, as implemented by Superintendent Sampson and the leadership team of Freehold Regional High School District, is to have observing groups take part in a role-alike jigsaw activity: One person from each group meets with observers from other groups. For example, all of the observers who focused on teacher look-fors from classroom observations meet together, all those who focused on students meet together, and so on. The new groups review evidence from their original teams' classroom observations and interviews. By developing patterns in this manner, it is less likely to link patterns to individual classrooms or interviewees.

Framing Wonderings. The groups also compile a small number of "wonderings" to share with the host leadership team. Like the patterns, wonderings emerge from the evidence collection and analysis; however, wonderings are not definitive statements but rather questions or concerns the group believes would be useful for the host leadership team to consider as it continues to explore its problem of practice or equity focus. For example, wonderings might ask how additional data, which observers did not have access to, might inform or relate to the evidence they did collect (e.g., How have the initiatives named in the look-fors impacted the ninth grade promotion data for Black and Latinx students?). Wonderings may direct attention to an issue of equity that had not been raised in the problem of practice or look-fors but for which the group had observed evidence. Wonderings also may come from the groups' knowledge of best practices in education (for example, How well is the school's adopted reading program suited to the needs of students learning English as an additional language?).

However they are framed, wonderings are intended to encourage the host leadership team to consider different aspects of the problem of practice or equity focus in relation to the school and/or district context. They support reflective practice by encouraging hosts to critically examine some of their initial assumptions. For Jersey City Public Schools, the wonderings focused on examining teacher beliefs associated with grouping and students' capacities for higher-order thinking, as identified in Figure 2.8.

Sharing Patterns and Wonderings. Toward the conclusion of their discussions, each group records its patterns and wonderings, either on chart paper or in a digital format (e.g., a Google form), and selects a spokesperson to briefly share them. Then, all the groups convene with the host leadership team. In some cases, the leadership team chooses to invite teachers whose classrooms have been visited; in others, teachers and other members of the school community will learn about the reports in later meetings.

The spokesperson from each group briefly (usually in just 2-3 minutes) shares their group's patterns and wonderings. At the end of each share-out, a facilitator asks for clarifying questions from the full group (including host team and school community members) but does

---

Figure 2.8   Sample Wonderings (Jersey City Public Schools)

- What's the difference between "grouping" and "group work"?
- Is there an imbalance between cultural work and rigor?
- How is the district addressing teacher beliefs related to students who may be lacking basic skills?
- Is basic skill mastery a prerequisite for higher-order thinking?

not allow more substantive discussion at this point. Clarifying questions might include asking how a small group defined a term such as "engagement," or for an example of evidence they collected related to a specific pattern. The patterns and wonderings remain posted for the final stage of the visit, Reflecting on the Next Steps of Equity-Focused Work, and remain with the host leadership team as artifacts for future discussions.

Step 3: Reflecting on the Next Steps of Equity-Focused Work

In this section, we consider some of the ways participants in equity visits reflect on their learning, first, in the moment, as part of the visit itself, and, later, in follow-up reflective activities. Reflection is meant both to support the host in formulating steps to address inequities and to expand observers' understanding of equity and instruction.

In-the-Moment Reflections

The patterns and wonderings provide the host school with a wealth of information, ideas, questions, and possibilities to help them move forward in addressing issues of equity—far more than can be processed in the short time left in the day's schedule. For this reason, the next segment of the visit schedule is intended only to initiate the more in-depth discussions that will take place over the following days, weeks, and months.

Two ways that NJNS has conducted reflections at the conclusion of an equity visit are using a fishbowl discussion and a next steps protocol. (See Appendix D for detailed descriptions of these protocols.) In selecting a protocol, host teams consider their goals, school and district culture, and needs.

Fishbowl Discussion. In a fishbowl discussion, representatives from the host leadership team convene in an inner circle, with observers sitting in a larger outer circle in order to "listen in" on the discussion. Typically facilitated by the superintendent or principal, inner-circle participants share their initial reflections on the day— what stood out to them, what surprised them, what they agreed with, and so on. Then, as a group, they begin to identify implications for their work going forward. This discussion generally lasts 30 to 40 minutes; it is deliberately framed as a time to brainstorm just a few possible action steps and/or areas for additional data collection rather than to draw conclusions or create a master strategy. It is intended to set the stage for additional meetings to review the patterns and wonderings more systematically. After the fishbowl discussion is over, and if time permits, observers outside of the circle have the opportunity to share their reflections or ask questions based on what they heard from the inner-circle discussion.

The fishbowl discussion during the equity visit to Jersey City high schools was facilitated by Superintendent Lyles. In the inner circle, host principals and central office administrators brainstormed some possible next steps and focus areas, including the following:

1. Make sure that the work is consistent and sustained—no one-shot deals.

2. Focus on inter-visitation both across departments within each school and across schools.

3. Identify best "practicers" (teachers already implementing the school's adopted best practices)—highlight and leverage the work of those teachers who are challenging students to use higher-order thinking.

4. Work across district lines by bringing coaches and others together to work on these issues.

5. Work on and decide on what "rigor" means.

Next Steps Protocol. This protocol calls on observers to brainstorm possible next steps for the host leadership team. Observers form small groups of three to five; these may be the same individuals who had collected data together, or a mix of participants from the earlier groups. The small groups identify potential action steps for the host related to its problem of practice and equity focus; these possible steps draw on the patterns and wonderings as resources. The groups formulate steps for three time frames: short term (e.g., what steps might be taken in the next month), medium term (within the next few months), and longer term (by the conclusion of the semester or year—about six months or so). Depending on when the visit takes place, the host leadership team and/or facilitators choose dates that make sense; for example, a visit held in October might include: (1) short term—last day of school before winter break, (2) medium term—last day of school before summer break, and (3) long term—first day of next school year.

While the groups are working, leadership team members and faculty from the host school may be invited to circulate among the groups and listen in as the groups formulate their suggestions. However, the hosts are cautioned by facilitators not to engage with the groups (and the observers not to engage with the hosts). In the full group, small groups briefly share out their suggestions, typically on chart paper with a brief (2–3 minute) verbal report. A member of the host leadership team, often the superintendent or principal, then briefly reflects on what they have heard. As with the fishbowl, the protocol is meant to generate ideas for future discussions, not resolve the problem of practice that drives the visit.

Individual Reflections on the Visit. The equity visit concludes with an opportunity for all the participants to reflect on their learning over the course of the day and to apply it to their own school and district contexts. This also provides an important opportunity for the learning community to reflect on its next steps, for example, for future equity visits or other activities.

Reflection may begin with the host team sharing their perspectives on the visit and then inviting perspectives of the observers. Some comments are likely to be technical in nature, for example, about how the schedule worked or might be adjusted to be more efficient; how well the amount of time spent in classrooms or interviews worked; and so on. Others address how effectively the specific look-fors allowed observers to collect evidence and address the problem of practice and equity focus—as well as issues of equity not identified within these.

Alongside the discussion, written reflections provide a crucial resource for observers and host leadership team members to share their perspectives, raise questions, and make suggestions for future visits. In NJNS, at the end of the visit or any meeting, all participants complete a one-page Learning Journal that prompts them to think about what they learned, what questions remain, and suggestions for future work. Figure 2.9 presents a collated sampling of learning journal responses from the equity visit to Jersey City (a learning journal template is included in the Appendix C).

These reflective activities often spark heated discussion within the group about equity and instruction. For example, after one equity visit, superintendents and leadership team members discussed how the teaching they had observed was similar to what they had seen in visits to other districts, irrespective of student demographics—and what this meant for underserved students no matter how poor or wealthy a district is. In another visit, participants shared struggles they have faced in confronting some faculty members' deficit beliefs about students' capacity to learn. These reflections allow observers to connect their experiences in the host schools with their work on equity in their own schools.

For the host leadership team, hearing that others are engaged in similar struggles provides moral and intellectual support for the work ahead. After the equity visit to high schools in her district, Superintendent Lyles reflected on her experience—how it affirmed her district's work, and how it challenged the leaders' understandings of providing all students with rigorous educational opportunities:

> *When asked to host an equity visit, my initial response was "No."*
> *I wasn't sure I was ready for outsiders to comment on our work.*

But I clearly remember the feeling of "Ahhh" at the end of the visit, with all of our warts exposed. After my leadership team left, the network got down to the real discussion about what had happened. We talked about the challenge of the "R word"—rigor. I remember most the observation from a design team member that spoke to the clear alignment that he observed across the four high schools to the district's theory of action and problem of practice around equity.

Figure 2.9   Sample Learning Journal Responses (Jersey City Public Schools)

What "aha" moments or insights did you have?

- It was instructive to witness the Problem of Practice in action. The school that I visited shared that the principal meets with department coordinators each week. Observing the honest reflection, cohesion, and constructive suggestions offered by the Jersey City team was inspiring and insightful. Engaging with leaders from multiple districts is invaluable.
- Large systems, 30K students, have layers of structures and complications in communications.
- Cultural development & improvements in instruction don't necessarily progress at an equal rate.
- There is a consistent tension between academic freedom and centralized expectations. This tension is necessary & vital to a healthy relationship between teachers and admin.

What remains unclear or what new questions do you have?

- How can we combat low teacher expectations in special education settings?
- Disconnect between expectations and level of rigor. . . .
- We still need definitions of rigor, engagement, collaboration, etc.
- How to close the gap between hopes and actuality.

How can we increase our individual and collective learning in future meetings?

- If possible, provide some more explicit parameters regarding expectations for look-fors. For example, how do we define "student discussion"?
- We must continue to examine this process through the lenses of the instructional core.
- Keep on, keeping on. . . .
- Would be wonderful to replicate visit a year, year/half from now. Perhaps we select students to be interviewed on next/subsequent visits.

Follow-Up Conversations

While the equity visit officially ends with final reflections, the work is not over. Follow-up conversations allow for the host leadership team to share the progress they have made since the equity visit. They also allow opportunity for extended conversations about ideas or questions that arose during the visit. For in-district equity visits, follow-up conversations likely involve the host principal and central office administrators; the host principal may also conduct follow-up conversations with teachers in their school. For cross-district equity visits, the host leadership team may report back their progress and questions at the following meeting of their network or learning community (see Chapter 3).

These follow-up conversations are essential, as they provide opportunities for deeper reflection and support the development of professional accountability (discussed in Chapter 3). In Jersey City Public Schools, for example, Superintendent Lyles requires principals to meet with central office administrators and use a Learning Together Consultancy protocol (see Appendix D) to debrief the visit and discuss next steps. Conducting these consultancies, she reports, has been "one of the most powerful pieces" of the equity visit process.

Within NJNS, participants reflect on each equity visit during the following month's meeting. The host leadership team share their reflections on the visit, what they have done so far to address the findings and wonderings, and what their next steps are. This provides an opportunity for additional feedback and reflections and also serves as an accountability measure for the host in taking action to address inequities. Whichever approach is used, the equity visit should be seen as just one in a series of activities meant to understand and confront inequities in students' experiences of school—not a single-day event that is "one and done."

PARTICIPANT REFLECTION

Asking Questions About Student Experiences Across Districts

Rachel Goldberg is an assistant superintendent in Passaic Public Schools and the former director of staff development at Elizabeth Public Schools, districts whose student populations are primarily low income and Latinx. In both districts, the superintendents are members of NJNS, and over the last 10 years, she has participated in equity visits to a range of diverse schools, many different from both of her districts. She reflects on how thinking about equity across district demographics helped her think further about equity and instruction in her own district.

Ultimately, our job as district leaders is to think about how members of this network can work together to identify how differences in student demographics appear in our school policies, culture, and classroom instruction. A key benefit of equity visits is looking at schools across the state to ask what instruction looks like for students in other districts. In the network, we sat across from districts very different from us, and we went and saw what their students experienced.

Having high-income, majority white districts in NJNS was fabulous for our learning. My team from Passaic looked at their practice as external points to better understand equity. The students attending those schools, what is their experience like? How do we duplicate that high-level instruction regardless of where the student goes to school?

Identifying an equity focus, collecting and analyzing data through an equity lens, and reflecting on the next steps represent the core elements for hosting a successful equity visit. Importantly, the first element occurs weeks before the actual visit, and the third element occurs weeks afterward, which affirms our understanding of equity visits as a practice that is most successful when embedded within an equity-focused learning community. In Vignette 1, we illustrate these steps in action by telling the story of an actual equity visit. In Chapter 3, we examine the purposes for such learning communities and some of the ways educational leaders organize them.

VIGNETTE 1

An Equity Visit to Appleton Elementary School

We now present an actual equity visit to give a better sense of what it looks like in practice. This visit took place in a district, Laurel Heights, that had already conducted several equity visits as part of the district's strategy to identify and address systemic inequities. It is not meant to be a model or template for equity visits, especially a first-time visit, but rather to illustrate what planning an equity visit involves and what a visit looks like "on the ground." The names of the district, school, and all staff members are pseudonyms in order to keep the individuals and district confidential, as the work is ongoing.

Identifying an Equity Focus:
Examining Mathematics Instruction at Appleton Elementary School

In Laurel Heights Public Schools, Superintendent Adam Jones had asked each principal to identify an equity focus and host an equity visit to investigate the focus, as part of the administrator professional development plan. The K–12 district serves about 8,500 students and has a long a history of high achievement. But Superintendent Jones knew that beneath the achievement results that were a source of pride across the community, pockets of inequity persisted, especially for Black and Latinx students, students living in poverty, and students receiving special education services. These student groups, however, were relatively small, and as a result, state-level data reports did not disaggregate their scores.

Naming the Equity Focus

In Year 3 of the equity visit process, it was finally Principal Sarah Turner's turn to host her fellow principals at her school, Appleton Elementary School. Principal Turner's first thought in identifying the school's equity focus was, "Anything but literacy. Five of the last six visits

(Continued)

(Continued)

focused on literacy problems. And I think all the principals had all decided that we couldn't go through another literacy issue again." Working with her school leadership team to analyze state achievement data, she discovered that mathematics in fact did pose greater challenges to students overall than literacy:

> *The mathematics scores this year were lower than they've ever been in the past. We always had significantly higher performance on state tests in mathematics and good performance, better than the district and certainly better than the state. This year, that wasn't the case. And that surprised us.*

At Appleton, over 80% of students were white. Because the numbers of students in other demographic categories, including Black, Latinx, English language learners (ELLs), and students receiving special education, were small, their group's performance was not reported with in the state test results. Thus Principal Turner could not just look at the state-created district or school report card. Instead, she needed to find another way to analyze the data to identify an equity focus. She began by making a list of all of the students who did not achieve proficiency on the state tests. She then made a spreadsheet identifying various characteristics of each of these students, including their race, gender, disability status, and so on. When she looked at the students with the 25 lowest scores, Principal Turner noted that they were overwhelmingly Black and Latinx, receiving special education services, and/or qualifying for free or reduced-price lunch.

To begin planning the equity visit, Principal Turner met with Superintendent Jones and a team of central office administrators. However, the superintendent had made it clear that the principals were to lead the equity work in their schools— as the key component of their leadership development plans (a state requirement). For that reason, most of the planning took place in Principal Turner's meetings with her school-based content specialists and teachers, along with the district's K–12 mathematics supervisor.

Formulating the Problem of Practice and Look-Fors

Now that Principal Turner and her team had identified their scope and equity focus—uneven performance in mathematics in the third grade—they developed a problem of practice for the visit:

> Performance of Appleton third and fourth grade students (as measured by state test performance levels) is significantly lower than the district averages for third and fourth grade performance in the area of mathematics. While this data trend exists for overall mathematics performance, closer analysis reveals that performance gaps between Appleton students in third and fourth grade who are considered to be at risk[2] (including a disproportionality of students of color) and overall district third and fourth grade students are greater in the area of mathematics.

---

[2]We use the term "at risk" in this vignette since it was a term common to Laurel Heights; later in the vignette, we share a discussion in which NJNS members challenged Superintendent Jones and his team about using this term.

Appleton School Equity Visit Look-Fors

Teacher:

- Teachers are asking questions.
- All adults in the room are engaged.
- Teachers are modeling mathematics processes.

Student:

- Students are asking questions for the purpose of understanding what they are doing.
- Students are actively engaged in mathematics conversations about the content they are learning.
- Students are active participants in small-group instruction, whole-class mini-lesson, individual conference, or independent mathematics work.

Content:

- Students have access to differentiated materials.
- Classroom has charts and/or displays that help students know or verbalize what they are accomplishing.
- Classroom displays include resources that encourage students to improve independent mathematics work.

The next step was for Principal Turner and her team to identify specific look-fors that would focus the observers on mathematics teaching and learning in classrooms.

The look-fors focused observers on instructional strategies the school and district had been working toward, including teacher modeling and differentiation, both of which had been a focus for professional development. Collectively, the look-fors were meant to attune the observers to the kinds of teaching and learning students were experiencing in mathematics classes. Collecting and analyzing data from across classrooms, Principal Turner hoped, would allow them to consider if different students had different types of access to the curriculum.

While the problem focused on third and fourth grade student performance, observers would visit mathematics classes at all levels. Principal Turner reasoned that students' learning in the higher grades was a result, at least in part, of their experiences in the earlier grades.

The team also developed a set of interview questions to elicit teachers' perspectives on the same problem of practice:

(Continued)

(Continued)

1. What do you think we at Appleton School should be doing to close the gap for students of color?

2. What do you do differently for students who are at risk? How do you know that your expectations in mathematics are appropriate?

3. How comfortable are you with the school-adopted materials for mathematics?

These questions focused observers on aspects of curriculum implementation and differentiation, as well as on how teacher expectations might be affecting students designated as "at risk" by the school. They mirrored the observation look-fors in relation to teachers' knowledge of mathematics and how they work to engage all students in their instructional practice.

Appleton School was now almost ready to host administrators from across the district. Before the visit, Principal Turner prepared a packet of materials for observers, including the agenda, the problem of practice, and recent state test data in mathematics disaggregated by performance level, race/ethnicity, economic disadvantage, and disability status. She also included several short articles related to instructional equity in mathematics that Superintendent Jones had shared with the district.

Organizing Administrators From Across the District for a Day of Learning

It is one thing to lead an elementary school full of children. It is another to coordinate a visit from almost 50 observers—not something we would recommend for a first equity visit! Unlike Laurel Heights's previous equity visits, this visit would include superintendents from NJNS. In addition to the over 25 Laurel Heights staff who attended a typical visit, over 20 NJNS members would come from districts across the state to participate in the equity visit.

In creating the schedule for the visit, Principal Turner and her team planned for nine groups of observers to conduct classroom observations and teacher interviews. In each group of six, there would be a facilitator/timekeeper, as well as two people paying attention to each role: teacher, student, and content. Each group included a mixture of Laurel Heights staff and NJNS members. Each group would visit four different classrooms for 15 minutes each; and each would interview a pair of teachers for 30 minutes.

The morning of the equity visit, observers entered the large gymnasium to find nine tables labeled with a group number and a continental breakfast along one wall. Each observer received a packet of materials including the agenda, the master schedule, the group role assignments, look-fors for each role, and interview questions, as well as information about the type of classrooms being visited—and of course, a school map. After a welcome by Principal Turner and Superintendent Jones, Principal Turner and her leadership team presented the problem of practice and shared data used to determine it. Then, observers were off to find their first classrooms.

Observing Mathematics Classes

As Group B entered, Ms. D had just asked students to erase their whiteboards and was presenting a new problem. "Okay, so you have a string that is 40 centimeters long. You cut it into pieces that are 10 centimeters each. How many pieces do you have? Remember to use pictures, words, or number models to show your thinking." Ms. D walked around the classroom, whispering quietly to one student who had not written anything down and observing the action on each student's whiteboard. After a few minutes, she continued, "Put your markers down. I see some good thinking. Does someone want to come to the board?"

A Black child raised his hand, and Ms. D called on him to go to the board. While the class watched, he began to draw out one long line and then broke it into three segments with two vertical lines. Ms. D watched silently as he looked at his work, and he quickly added an additional vertical line to create four segments. "Good checking," she observed, and asked the class, "Did you notice what he did?"

A white student called out, "He put four."

Ms. D asked, "The first time, what did he have?"

Students: "He had three, then he corrected it."

Ms. D then asked the original student, "Why did you change it?" followed by, "Can you represent it as a number model?"

The student wrote, "10 × 4."

Group B's facilitator looked at the clock and nodded to the observers, who then quietly left the room. During the five-minute "hallway huddle," they each shared one piece of evidence that they observed. One observer focusing on the teacher noted, "She asks the students to explain their answers." Another focused on students: "All students had attempted a solution on their whiteboard. Some drew pictures and others wrote out the problem." A third observer, focused on content, stated that having individual whiteboards meant every student could attempt the problem and easily correct mistakes, which many students did.

The group proceeded to Ms. L's first-grade classroom, in which students each had a worksheet with several number lines printed on it. Most of the students were following along a number line divided by 1s, drawing an arc between each number with their pencil while saying each number aloud (see Figure 2.9). Ms. L was doing the same thing at the large board at the front of the classroom.

Figure 2.9 Student Counting Hops on the Number Line

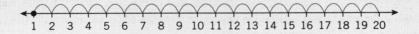

The students counted together: "15, 16, 17, 18, 19, 20."

Ms. L asked: "If we kept counting, what number would be next?"

(Continued)

(Continued)

Several students shouted out, "21!"

Ms. L reminded students, "Keep drawing your hops." Counting hops, as Group B learned, is an approach to teaching students how to use a number line as a way to skip count, initially counting by 1s, and then moving on to count by 2s, 5s, and so on. As Ms. L circled the classroom, she noticed that several students had gone ahead on their worksheets, and she silently and quickly erased the work they had done.

She then continued the lesson. "Let's take a look at the next one. Can someone read the directions?" After a white girl read the directions, Ms. L asked, "What number do we start with?" The student suggested, "5."

Ms. L responded, "We always start with 0. If I hop 10 hops, where do I hop to?" She called a different child, a white boy, to the board to solve the problem of counting hops by 10. He began to draw out his number line and his "hops." When Ms. L saw that he had made a mistake, she erased his work and asked him, "How many hops are we counting? Don't draw it yet. Count by 1s to get to 10. If we take one giant hop, where would we land?"

Again, Group B's facilitator got the observers' attention, and they returned to the hallway. One teacher observer noted, "Ms. L erased students' work on their worksheets and on the board and did not ask them to explain their incorrect answers." A student observer noted, "One student wanted to start counting from 5, which is mathematically possible." Finally, a content observer reported, "A large number line is displayed on the board that all students could see."

Interviewing Teachers

After observing two more classrooms, Group B returned to the gymnasium to meet with two teachers, Ms. M and Ms. B. Using the interview questions in the packet, group members asked teachers for their perspectives on the disproportionate number of students of color identified as "at risk" and what the school was doing to address this concern.

Ms. M began, "Mathematics is language-based. Our Latino and Indian students don't have a strong language base, so we simplify the language we use and focus on vocabulary. We have to break things down. The homework that is part of the mathematics curriculum is too complicated because it's language-based, and parents can't help them."

Ms. B added, "We support students, especially special education students, by supplementing the adopted curriculum with other worksheets so that parents will be able to help the kids at home."

Since the teachers both had experience in co-teaching classrooms, a member of Group B asked, "What do you do differently for students receiving special education services?"

Ms. B said, "With special education students, we take longer with each lesson. We need to break down the skills into manageable units. We break down word problems into steps."

Ms. M reflected, "We should have different tests. Special education kids shouldn't be counted in the count for the state tests."

The teachers agreed, "The curriculum we adopted is not for special education kids. It won't get them to meet standards." "For special education students," the teachers added, "we need to work with them on basic skills before they can move on to some of the more advanced strategies in the curriculum."

Ms. M's final thoughts brought the group back to standardized testing, "Our kids are making progress, but they still don't pass the tests. Our school's internal benchmark assessments are artificially inflated so the kids do fine on those. On these assessments, we simplify the wording and give support, and we can't do that for the state tests, so our kids struggle."

The members of Group B thanked the teachers for their time and perspectives and then went back to the gym for a quick lunch before analyzing their data and relating it to Appleton School's problem of practice.

Developing Patterns and Wonderings

The nine groups met again at their assigned tables and began to analyze the data they had collected from the observations and interviews. Group B began with each observer answering "yes" or "no" to the presence of the look-fors for the category they were assigned. For example, one student look-for asked, "Were students asking questions for the purpose of understanding what they are doing?" The two observers who had the student observer role addressed this, determining that in one of the four classes, they had seen evidence of students asking these types of questions.

For the look-for, "teachers modeling mathematics processes, or encouraging mathematics thinking," there was more discussion and disagreement. One observer asked, "Would it count as 'yes' if the teacher is posing questions and encouraging students to answer the questions?" After some discussion, the group decided that they would only say "yes" if the teacher asked questions that required students to explain their thinking in relation to how they solved a problem, using the example of the lesson on dividing the string into four pieces. In contrast, they decided, the lesson on "hopping" along the number line did not show evidence that the teacher encouraged students to explain their answers, figure out why things worked, or even understand why they always start from 0 when counting. After tabulating their findings in an online form provided by the hosts, the group reflected on both the look-fors and interview responses to develop a set of wonderings.

As the small groups finished charting their wonderings, Appleton staff members, including teachers who were interviewed and whose classes were visited, began to enter the gym. A member of the host leadership team collated the tabulations of look-for reports from all the small groups and made these into bar graphs, one for each look-for, to demonstrate how many times a specific look-for was observed across all of the observing groups.

The report out to whole group, including the host leadership team and Appleton staff members, began with a slide show of the bar graphs with data on the look-fors. These were first reported one look-for at a time. For example, Figure 2.10 shows that of the nine small groups (labeled A through I), seven saw some evidence of active participation in small groups, and three saw evidence of this in all four of the classrooms they visited. Then the team projected the same look-for data but organized by role (student, teacher, content). Figure 2.11 demonstrates that there were 12 observations of students asking questions, 12 of active engagement, and 17 of active participation in small-group instruction, all out of a possible 36 observations (nine small groups that each visited 4 classrooms).

(Continued)

(Continued)

Figure 2.10   Sample Pattern Reporting for One Look-For (Laurel Heights School District)

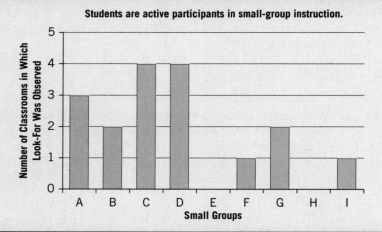

Students are active participants in small-group instruction.

Figure 2.11   Sample Pattern Reporting for One Category (Laurel Heights School District)

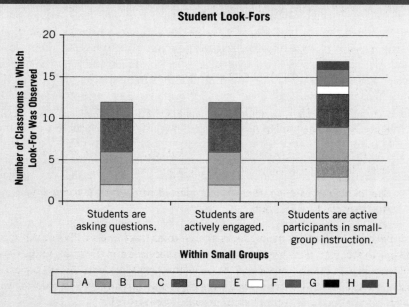

Student Look-Fors

Next, the small groups shared the wonderings they had recorded on large pieces of poster paper. Group B, for example, offered, "How is content differentiated?" "Are assessments being used to modify instruction for low-performing and high-performing students?" "Are the needs of at risk students being met?" As the other groups followed suit, themes emerged—about teachers' conceptual mathematics knowledge and how it affected their instruction; how students were grouped; how curriculum and instruction were differentiated to meet different students' current levels of performance; and whether some Appleton staff members had low expectations for students from some of the targeted groups, especially students with disabilities and students learning English as an additional language.

The nature of these types of wonderings likely made at least some Appleton teachers and staff members uncomfortable. However, they also had the potential to provoke new ideas for the school and district.

Reflecting on the Next Steps of Equity-Focused Work: Moving Forward (and Looking Back)

It was now time for Appleton School staff to reflect on what they heard and for observers to consider how their observations and reflections might inform their own practice.

Fishbowl Conversation

Principal Turner and seven teachers formed a circle in the center of the room, surrounded by other Laurel Heights staff and NJNS members. The conversation moved quickly to how students learning English as an additional language and students receiving special education services were able to engage with the mathematics curriculum adopted by the district.

Teacher 1: *The patterns that everyone found make me think we need to have more conversations about mathematics with our students.*

Teacher 2: *Yes, but don't our ELLs need to learn content vocabulary first? How can they play the mathematics games if they can't speak English?*

Teacher 1: *Maybe if we could have more space to post vocabulary around the room, so they could see the words?*

Teacher 3: *I don't know. The kids' language is so low. Even if they are thinking about mathematics, they can't write out what they think.*

Teacher 4: *I agree for special ed kids. I wonder if the kids who are pulled out of our classrooms for things like speech therapy could practice mathematics content there.*

Teacher 3: *Special ed kids can't get through our adopted curriculum. It uses too much language that they can't understand.*

In this snippet of conversation, the teachers shared their frustration with how little time they had to work with students receiving special education services and those learning English as an additional language. Some also expressed the belief that these students did not have the capacity to master the adopted curriculum. They went on to discuss some next steps they could take individually and as a school to support students who were struggling.

Teacher 3: *I think we should look at the schedule again and how we are using time to make sure all kids are getting access to all parts of the curriculum. If special education kids are always missing the games, they won't really get the full curriculum.*

(Continued)

Teacher 7: *Then maybe we could make like a mathematics boot camp, with intensive drill for kids who really need it, but put it in the schedule somewhere so the kids aren't missing key lessons.*

Teacher 1: *I think we also need to work on our understanding of mathematics. Sometimes I don't really get the reason for some of the games in the curriculum, so when the kids play them, I'm never quite sure how I should be helping or what's the point.*

Teacher 2: *Right. Are we giving kids misconceptions about big ideas in mathematics because we aren't mathematics specialists? More professional development on actual content would really help us understand the curriculum.*

Principal Turner closed the fishbowl discussion, thanking her teachers for opening their classrooms to district administrators and NJNS observers. She highlighted key themes that stood out to her, especially around structural change and mathematics content knowledge, as focus areas for the school's next steps. Superintendent Jones and facilitators from NJNS added their appreciation for staff members and students.

Observer Reflections on the Day

After Appleton staff departed, NJNS observers remained for a final discussion about the visit. Superintendent Jones began by reflecting that while all teachers said they have high expectations for all students, some did not believe every child they taught could meet standards. Overall, a pattern existed of lower expectations for some students, especially students learning English as an additional language and students receiving special education services.

NJNS members echoed this concern. One member noted that he had observed in one of the pullout classes for special education, all of the students were children of color. The group discussed how this raised questions of racial disproportionality in special education placement. Another NJNS member's comments returned the group to questions of expectations, deficit beliefs, and language.

> *I have come to this experience today not wanting my children to be children "at risk" anymore. I want my children to be children "at promise." If you look at me as a child-at-promise, you will see me differently than a child-at-risk. Language is important. Language can give credence to belief structures or challenge them . . . in our group interviews, [we heard teachers say] "Families are to blame, that if only we had better families, like the families we used to have, then we would be able to do this. We can't close the gap because some families don't bring to the table what our other families bring."*

The group discussed how using "at risk" in framing of the equity visit reinforces implicit biases that Appleton educators have about some students.

Several NJNS members shared their observations of Black and Latinx students and students learning English as an additional language from the morning's classroom visits:

"I know for one student who made a mistake, a Black boy, neither teacher corrected him."

"I observed an African American girl sit there not participating."

"We had similar experience with English language learners. They were just sitting not utilizing manipulatives."

These observations led the group to reflect on the process of creating patterns based on look-fors: The quantitative tabulation led to the quick, visual identification of the frequency of look-fors but did not allow them to share observations like those above. Members also noted that, for the teacher interviews, teachers might have been less candid knowing that they could be identified by a school or district staff member who knew which group interviewed which teachers. A design team member suggested using the following network meeting to address these process critiques. Superintendent Jones said that he would report back to NJNS the results of his follow-up conversations with Principal Turner, including the conversation in which he raised the concern about the term "at risk."

Following Up With Central Office and Teacher Leaders

In the week following the visit, Principal Turner met with Lana Spiegel, an experienced mathematics teacher at Appleton, and organized the wonderings into a single document to share with the full faculty. She stated that their staff had found the visit valuable and that the trust she had with her staff enabled them to hear the feedback as constructive and not critical.

Six weeks later, at the next NJNS meeting, Superintendent Jones, Principal Turner, and several Laurel Heights teachers and administrators shared with the network their reflections on the visit and their next steps. Two of the key questions raised for them by the visit related to students' level of engagement in mathematics classes and the extent to which lower expectations for some students might be affecting instruction. Principal Turner reported that she had since brought in additional academic support teachers. She had also reviewed the school's process for identifying students who need additional support.

One of the Appleton teachers commented that the visit "increased my awareness that there is an equity imbalance. . . . Now I'm really reflecting on my practice and asking if I'm reaching everyone effectively." Superintendent Jones also talked about expectations and what he can do to address teachers' and administrators' expectations across the district, suggesting that "If a teacher doesn't feel in their heart that every student can do it, then everything is window dressing."

This vignette illustrates an actual equity visit to an actual school within a district struggling to address long-standing inequities that had been hidden to many. Rather than a model for an ideal visit, this vignette shows some of the types of conversations that are possible when leaders commit to investigating intersections of equity and instruction, in this case in elementary school mathematics. One reason these types of conversations have pushed forward the work of Appleton School, as noted by its principal, is the foundation of relational trust within the school and the professional accountability and reflective practice that are parts of administrative culture in Laurel Heights. Creating a learning community that fosters such a culture is the focus of Chapter 3.

CHAPTER THREE

EQUITY-FOCUSED LEARNING COMMUNITIES

> *The growth of any craft depends on shared practice and honest dialogue among the people who do it. We grow by private trial and error, to be sure—but our willingness to try, and fail, as individuals is severely limited when we are not supported by a community that encourages such risks.*
>
> —Parker Palmer, American Author,
> Educator, and Activist

Equity-focused leadership is challenging. It requires core beliefs and principles that often are at odds with those that perpetuate the current reality in schools. Equity-focused leaders engage in ongoing efforts to introduce and sustain system-wide policies, practices, and reforms that run counter to commonly held beliefs about education, particularly for underserved students.

For individuals to lead for equity, being part of a community of like-minded colleagues provides encouragement, inspiration, support, challenge, learning, and growth. Across the United States, educational leaders are often isolated in their work (Daresh & Alexander, 2015). For equity-focused leaders, the isolation is likely to be even greater. These leaders have little opportunity to interact with other colleagues interested in developing the professional knowledge and skills necessary to advance educational equity in their districts and schools.

In this chapter, we define three key features of an equity-focused learning community, one that supports initiatives such as equity visits: relational trust, reflective practice, and professional accountability. We also describe three core organizational capacities—planning, facilitation, and documentation—for a learning community that models these features. Each one of these entails a range of tools that supports the work, especially norms, protocols, and templates (see Figure 3.1). These features and capacities can serve as a foundation for educational leaders to develop their own equity-focused communities within or across district contexts.

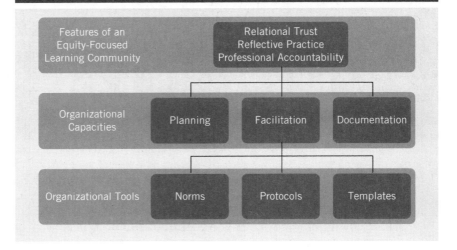

Figure 3.1 Developing an Equity-Focused Learning Community

LEARNING ABOUT EQUITY IN A COMMUNITY

The fundamental rationale for a learning community is simple but powerful: When multiple minds are brought to address a complex problem, both individual and collective learning is enhanced (Laughlin, Hatch, Silver, & Boh, 2006). According to Theoharis (2007), sustained interactions with peers support equity-focused leaders in multiple ways:

- Facilitating the acquisition of new knowledge and skills related to identifying inequities within instructional practice

- Providing examples of successful equity-focused strategies and initiatives that address systemic inequities while supporting high levels of performance for all students

- Providing resources for developing and implementing these equity-focused policies and practices

- Creating a space for leaders to get critical feedback on their work in an environment characterized by relational trust

- Inspiring and motivating leaders to address the various challenges they face, especially when they are isolated in their school or district contexts

Learning communities can bring a group's collective intelligence to bear on entrenched systemic inequities. They also provide inspiration and moral support for leaders who may face resistance within their own schools and districts. As former superintendent of the School District of South Orange and Maplewood, Brian Osborne observed, "While I am alone in my district, I know from the conversations in this group that I'm not alone in my desire to advance equity for all students."

PARTICIPANT REFLECTION

Becoming Part of an "Educational Think Tank"

Until her retirement, Superintendent Jacqueline Young led the Essex Regional Educational Services Commission, a small regional district serving students who underperformed on state tests and functioned significantly below grade level. Most students in her district received special education services, and many had experienced trauma and had behavioral challenges. One of the district's schools was located in a juvenile detention center. The students were mostly male, poor, and Black or Latinx.

This student population was quite different from almost all of the other districts whose superintendents were in NJNS. In her reflection, she discusses some of the key features of a learning community explored in this chapter, a shared commitment, relational trust, and professional accountability that connected leaders across diverse district types.

For me, the network was a lot of things. It was a source of inspiration. If I needed to be injected with something to keep going, it was my injection. I looked forward to it every month, just to interact with my colleagues, then to visit their districts. Seeing the different initiatives they were using and how they were addressing their own issues, that gave me inspiration. It gave me the sense that I could do better, because I had seen what was working in other places. If it was working there—it may not look the same for me— but I could take it and modify it for my district.

The network was also a place to share my expertise. This year, by inviting my network colleagues to have an equity visit at Sojourn High School [a high school within a juvenile detention center], they saw that I really am doing the work. After the equity visit, people told me, "Whatever you're doing that's successful with the kids, whatever you're doing that you see that helps them to be focused, maybe you could chronicle that and give us feedback as to what we need to do in our districts to support kids in difficult situations."

The network was like a think tank. We shared ideas, we visited each other's districts, and we talked about things that were problematic for us in our own districts and problems across all of our districts. We felt comfortable sharing with each other because of the norms that we had established. We had trust that we could say things in the network, concerns about our districts, and know that what we said wouldn't be repeated outside. All of us strived to take ideas from the network and implement them. Everyone's situation is a little bit different, and every district has different equity goals, but we are all superintendents who really feel the importance of doing this work.

The network is a group of leaders with a shared commitment. The fact that we have been together for a period of time says that we're committed to our purpose. We could relate to each other beyond our meetings, and there was a sense that we were really there to assist each other and all of our kids. I may have waited until the last minute to do an assignment for a network meeting. But I knew that even if I had to stay up late the night before, I would not walk in there on Friday without having done what I was supposed to do.

Learning in Community From Equity Visits

As we described in Chapter 2, planning and conducting an effective equity visit is complex project that requires dedicated time and the involvement of many people, from the superintendent or principal and their leadership teams, to teachers and professional staff in schools, to students. While the equity visit itself is a highly visible event meant to serve as a catalyst for change, it needs to be related to the ongoing professional learning of its participants and their day-to-day responsibilities as educational leaders. Stand-alone learning experiences, such as a conference, workshop, or speaker, are unlikely to create systemic change.

Equity visits, by contrast, are meant to be part of participants' ongoing learning. They model the qualities of effective professional development for educational leaders; that is, they are long-term, job-embedded, and focused on student learning and they provide opportunities for reflection (Peterson, 2002; Sparks & Hirsch, 2000). At a minimum, equity visits are book-ended by planning and debrief meetings. Planning meetings involve host leadership teams in reviewing data, identifying a problem of practice and equity focus, and determining which classrooms to visit and other evidence to review. Debrief meetings are structured opportunities for host leadership team members to share what they have learned and create professional accountability for action (discussed later in this chapter).

Integrating equity visits into the professional life of educational leaders requires effort. It calls for continual monitoring to ensure that the focus remains squarely on equity and instruction. It also requires managing organizational tasks so that participants in the community are engaged in supporting one another's learning. Equity-focused learning communities vary in many ways, depending on their organization and membership (e.g., in-district or cross-district, member characteristics, size, external partner or consultant). However, their core features are well established in the literature on professional learning communities; these include ongoing collaboration among participants, reflective dialogue, and collective responsibility for preK–12 students' learning as well as for one another's professional learning (Grossman, Wineburg, & Woolworth 2001; Little, 2007; Stevens & Kahne, 2006; Stoll & Louis, 2007).

Equity-focused learning communities, like NJNS, connect these core features to a fundamental commitment to examining and addressing inequities in students' educational experiences, opportunities, and outcomes. Together, participants in such a community identify and act on inequities that other educational leaders may avoid. In taking on these challenges as a community, participants build shared knowledge, develop common practices, and apply their learning in their own unique organizational contexts. To be effective as learning communities, especially ones taking on issues of equity and race, participants commit to three core values: relational trust, reflective practice, and professional accountability.

Developing Relational Trust

Trust is the foundation for a community of educational leaders to openly and effectively address inequities that harm students of color and other underserved students within their school contexts. Doing this type of work involves confronting complex personal and societal beliefs. It also demands a level of vulnerability on the leader's part that is rarely exposed in their professional life. Superintendent Jorden Schiff referred to NJNS as a learning community that "keeps me honest. It keeps me questioning: 'Have I done enough today for the kids that need my best decision-making the most? Have I done good work today, and have I challenged the conventional wisdom enough?'" For Schiff, as for other participants, NJNS has provided the critical feedback to initiate a number of approaches to supporting underperforming groups of students in his high-performing district.

Trust is necessary for creating and sustaining conditions that support inquiry and vulnerability. Bryk and Schneider (2003) define relational trust in schools as "an interrelated set of mutual dependencies [that] are embedded within the social exchanges in any school community" (p. 41). For Bryk and Schneider, relational trust is characterized by respect, personal regard, competence in core role responsibilities, and personal integrity. Without such trust, schools are unlikely to engage in meaningful change efforts.

When Superintendent Marcia Lyles introduced racial autobiographies to her principals in Jersey City Public Schools, she did so with an awareness of the district's history of avoiding explicit discussions of race. To build the trust required for the principals to take part, she began by asking for volunteers to share their work. She explicitly told principals that whatever they had to say would be welcome, even if she did not personally agree with it.

The first principal who spoke shared his belief that "race doesn't matter in Jersey City." This color-neutral philosophy ran counter to the very goal of Superintendent Lyles' initiative. However, rather than criticizing him, she publicly acknowledged his belief as *his* truth: "One tenet we agreed to is that each autobiography is someone's truth, and we have to respect that. It may not be mine or yours, but that is his truth." A few years later, Superintendent Lyles noted, this same principal wrote her to say that he now "finally and wholeheartedly got" what she was trying to do in having administrators talk about race.

Educational leaders play a key role in fostering relational trust by listening to and valuing what others have to say and by modeling expectations that others do so as well. Leaders set a tone that recognizes the unique experiences individuals bring to the work. They model and encourage a climate of risk taking and openness. Principal Brian Donahue, of the Freehold Regional High School District, described how Superintendent Sampson shared the findings from an equity visit in the district with his leadership team:

> *[The superintendent] was great about sharing with us that whatever came out of the visit was not evaluative. That this was for our growth. And he really did live that. If your superintendent doesn't live that and doesn't allow that process to take place, the equity visit is just another thing that people put on a dog-and-pony show for. Trust really does start at the top, and we felt like the critical feedback we got from the equity visit was an opportunity for growth.*

Building Reflective Practice

School and district leaders typically have few places to reflect on their practice with colleagues and peers, and even fewer that target reflection on issues of equity. That is not surprising: Working to change the status quo in terms of race and education in the United States requires administrators and others to reflect on their own implicit biases and assumptions, as well as to support teachers and other professionals in doing so (Oakes, Lipton, Anderson, & Stillman, 2015).

Argyris and Schön (1974) demonstrate that everyone engaged in decision making maintain two theories that are often at odds: an "espoused theory," how they describe to others what they are doing, and a "theory-in-use," what they are actually doing. Typically, Argyris (1977) maintains, "they do not *use* the theories they explicitly espouse" (p. 119). In order to improve, adjust, or even eliminate ineffective practices, leaders need to make their theories-in-use explicit so that their theories-in-use and espoused theories are more closely aligned.

In an equity-focused learning community, participants regularly develop and reflect on their espoused theories and their theories-in-use. They strive to understand how their theories guide their day-to-day decisions; and they get feedback from colleagues on the alignment between the two kinds of theories. In NJNS, participating superintendents and leadership team colleagues regularly share their ongoing work related to identifying equity focus areas, along with data that were used to frame them, and receive critical feedback from colleagues. This practice occurs not only in preparation for an equity visit but as ongoing professional learning experience for all participants.

Building in specific opportunities for reflective practices transforms equity visits from a one-day event into a regular part of their work. Sustained work on equity means that learning and reflection begin before an equity visit and continue afterward.

Principals in Jersey City Public Schools highlighted the importance of this built-in time for reflection both during equity visits and in the weeks following a visit. When the district initially implemented equity visits, there was no formal follow-up to the daylong visit. Principals rarely shared their takeaways after a visit, nor did they have meetings with their colleagues or supervisors to discuss potential changes in practice or policy. To keep the learning from equity visits at the forefront, Superintendent Lyles required a follow-up meeting for host principals to reflect on the visit and meant their next steps. The district also provided release time for those who had observed at a school to meet with the host principal a few weeks following the visit to debrief and discuss next steps.

Creating Professional Accountability

For teachers, professional accountability comes "through opportunities for public practice, joint planning, and review of practice" (Darling-Hammond, 1989, p. 38). In teachers' professional learning communities, participants open their classroom doors to colleagues and provide feedback to one another on their teaching and students' learning. In doing so, they take on shared responsibility for each other's professional learning and instructional improvement.

Educational leaders, typically, have fewer demands for—and opportunities to practice—a similar degree of professional accountability. More often, they are guided by bureaucratic accountability, which involves addressing federal, state, or district mandates and policies (Khalifa, Jennings, Briscoe, Oleszweski, & Abdi, 2014). Principals are held accountable by their superintendents, superintendents by state departments of education and school boards—with standardized assessments the primary measure of success. Even without explicit and binding mandates and policies to guide them, leaders are often influenced by their perceptions of what will satisfy powerful stakeholders, whether these be direct superiors, school board members, or influential community groups. These forms of accountability discourage initiatives that challenge the status quo, including those that would benefit students and groups who have been historically underserved.

Equity-focused learning communities counter bureaucratic accountability by placing equity at the center of the leader's decision making and action taking. As in teachers' learning communities, educational leaders make their practices public to one another. They share data, initiatives, progress, and obstacles. They invite critical feedback from peers on how they are identifying and addressing inequities in their schools. Superintendent Hayes describes the professional accountability developed through NJNS as a network that "both gives me inspiration and invokes guilt. It's not a burdensome guilt," but it has pushed her to stay committed to the equity focus. "It is very challenging to always remain focused. You get pulled off task.

An equity-focused learning community supports professional accountability by creating a shared sense of urgency about the systemic inequities that participants are committed to addressing. It helps leaders recognize the ways that inequities may be hidden in how data are reported or in how schools or districts are held accountable by state mandates.

Cross-district learning communities may find it easier, at least initially, to develop professional accountability because participants choose to join, already committed to the equity focus. In NJNS, new superintendents understand the expectations for publicly identifying and addressing a district inequity with their colleagues, and eventually hosting an equity visit in their district. In his first year in NJNS, Superintendent Rocco Tomazic of Freehold Borough Schools already valued critical feedback from his NJNS colleagues.

> *There have been a number of times that at different places, the more experienced superintendents have given me an insight or a correction, not a put-down . . . a calibration, that's the word I'm looking for—a calibration of my thinking, almost like a self-correction. We self-correct each other.*

In-district learning communities pose different challenges to ensure administrators' participation. Mandating participation may appear to be the most efficient way to get the work under way; however, doing so may create a new type of bureaucratic accountability; that is, administrators may participate because they have to, not because they find the work meaningful. Superintendent Lyles's approach to racial autobiographies, described earlier, offers one way to both require that everyone participate in equity-focused work and allow individuals to enter the discussion as they are ready to do so. This can lessen bureaucratic demands and create space for leaders to develop their own sense of accountability to their colleagues.

PARTICIPANT REFLECTION

Being Bound Together and Held to Task

Kenyon Kummings, Superintendent of Wildwood Public Schools, joined NJNS in its ninth year. He reflects on how the network pushed him to advance equity work in his district.

I came in to the network, and I was very excited. Initially, I was trying to figure out where my district's place was in the network. As I got to know people, I got a sense that we're all on a continuum of equity work. I gained a stronger understanding of what I should be doing locally, in my district, from conversations with others about their district work. It never felt like an exercise just to be compliant.

There is a healthy level of peer pressure in the network too. There are a lot of distractors when you get back to the district, all these other things that impact you and try to pull your attention away from focusing on equity. Sometimes it feels inconvenient to be doing something with the network every month, but at the same time, knowing that everybody is in this together, it's like we are bound together. Whatever we might be doing at a network meeting, I know that I have to come prepared to the meeting, because there is going to be some opportunity where we are going to share our progress in our districts. And that is just enough to make sure I am prepared to share.

I am glad to know that I'm going to be held to task. I like the peer pressure; it keeps pushing us forward to keep working on things.

PUTTING TOGETHER ORGANIZATIONAL COMPONENTS OF SUSTAINED LEARNING COMMUNITIES

Initiating and maintaining equity-focused learning communities that demonstrate relational trust, reflective practice, and professional accountability, whether in-district or cross-district, requires ongoing attention and support. In this section, we describe three overlapping capacities that provide guidance and support to the community: planning, facilitation, and documentation. Each involves a team of people whose roles may overlap as well as complement one another. We also highlight some of the tools we have used in NJNS to support each of the capacities.

Planning Equity Visits

As we described in Chapter 2, a single equity visit involves a great deal of planning. The planning is even more when equity visits are an ongoing and central practice part of a learning community. A planning team is required to manage the work, with two key responsibilities: (1) holding the vision for equity-focused learning and (2) ensuring that all activities align with that vision. The team considers how each equity visit will contribute to participants' professional learning and how each visit is contextualized within a yearlong series of activities that extend and deepen the learning from individual visits; these activities may include identifying equity focus areas, analyzing data, discussing research articles, inviting speakers, and so on. While multiple individuals will be involved in the planning, having a dedicated program manager or point person can make the coordination of the team members' time and efforts more feasible.

A planning team for an in-district community consists of several individuals, generally with leadership positions within the district; these might include assistant superintendents, principals, and/or instructional specialists. This team plans equity visits and other meetings that support the district's equity work. It also provides the ongoing coordination and communication required to make the visits a regular professional practice within the district. This includes creating schedules for the year, planning visits and events, allocating resources, and maintaining regular communication with all stakeholders in the initiative.

Typically, the superintendent identifies the planning team members and plays an active role on the team. Creating a functioning team may require redefining central office administrators' and principals' professional job descriptions so that they can take on new responsibilities. It is likely that the workload changes will be most significant in the initial stages of the work. In Hillsborough Township Public Schools, for instance, Superintendent Schiff worked closely with his principals in the early years to plan in-district school visits. Over time, principals have taken on much of the work for hosting an equity visit at their school, and the superintendent is only minimally involved.

Planning for cross-district learning communities is likely to be more complex, since participants from different districts are involved. Superintendent Victoria Kniewel, then of West Windsor-Plainsboro Regional School District, highlighted the challenge of maintaining a cross-district group of superintendents: "I remember trying to start a network a couple different times in my career. It was never sustainable. No one has time to add planning to their busy schedule, and it falls apart because there is not a shared understanding of vision."

In NJNS, thanks to the support of external funders and membership dues, we have been fortunate to have a design team of experienced practitioners and researchers to coordinate the work. The design team meets monthly to reflect on the previous meeting and plan the upcoming ones. While some planning meetings take place in person, most are conducted as conference calls and take advantage of document-sharing technology. Much of the discussion in these meetings addresses logistics of planning and communication; we also continually raise questions about how the work is maintaining a focus on equity and instruction.

Most cross-district learning communities will not have this type of support. Instead they may create a smaller planning team or one with rotating leadership to work with hosts of upcoming visits and plan other meetings of the community. In such a case, it will be important for all members to continually reflect on how the community's work supports their learning about equity and instruction. Sometimes it is possible to identify an individual from a local university or professional development organization to fill this role. As long as the community members are committed to the work, one external program manager or logistics coordinator can provide the support needed for this type of professional learning.

Facilitating Equity Visits

Planning provides the overall frame for a year's focus on equity and structures for individual meetings. Ensuring that the discussions and activities that occur during the meetings reflect the qualities of an equity-focused learning community—relational trust, reflective practice, and professional accountability—also requires diligent and thoughtful facilitation.

The facilitator of a learning community has two main responsibilities: to support the group in a discussion (or activity) that addresses its intended purposes and to create and maintain a climate for inclusion, collaboration, and critical thinking. While facilitators do not dominate the discussion, they step in as needed to make sure that the discussion stays focused and to allow all participants opportunities to share their perspectives. These facilitation responsibilities are especially important in discussions of race and equity, particularly in communities with participants of different racial and ethnic backgrounds—a topic we explore in greater detail in Chapter 4. Facilitators must be open to engaging with difficult, even uncomfortable, discussions about these topics. This requires that they critically reflect on their own facilitation.

Facilitators are often members of the planning team but may include others from the learning community who volunteer to facilitate a specific activity or discussion. For example, within NJNS, it is common for experienced superintendents to facilitate a small group during classroom visits and interviews. For in-district communities, facilitators might include assistant superintendents and curriculum supervisors, external professional development providers or coaches, or teacher leaders. Facilitators are supported in this work by a number of tools, described below, including group norms and discussion protocols.

Documenting Equity Visits

Documentation, the third capacity in supporting a thriving learning community, is easily overlooked; however, documenting equity visits and other activities within the community supports the learning of individuals and the community about equity and instruction. In practical terms, it eases the work of planning and preparing for visits and other meetings, as it provides a bank of existing agendas, protocols, look-fors, and other resources to adapt and build upon. More substantially, it provides resources for the double-loop learning described above: ongoing reflection on the community's practices and learning, especially about the interaction of equity and instruction.

Many aspects of an equity visit might be documented; chief among these are as follows:

- The equity focus and problem of practice of each equity visit

- Patterns and wonderings developed by the small groups (often recorded on chart paper or a shared online document)

- Notes from small- or large-group conversations during equity visits

- Participants' written and/or oral reflections at the end of meetings (individual and consolidated, e.g., on a flipchart or in a digital format)

It is also useful to document certain parts of planning and debrief meetings. During a discussion of an upcoming equity visit, the host typically asks for feedback on the emerging problem of practice and look-fors. If this feedback is recorded on chart paper, this artifact can be photographed or transcribed. Written reflections during the meeting can be collected as well.

NJNS was fortunate to have the support of university-based researchers recruited to document network activity, which allowed for deep documentation of every meeting and visit, as well as an annual survey of and interviews with members. These sources of data were critical in the discussions within the design team and NJNS as a whole that shaped the evolution to more explicit equity-focused work, including the creation of equity visits. However, this level of documentation is not necessary for successful equity visit practice. Documentation can be done informally and with fewer resources. For example, facilitators can collect participants' written reflections at the end of a meeting, patterns and wonderings recorded on chart paper can be photographed with a cell phone camera for later transcription, and so on.

As important as the efforts to document the community's discussions is the commitment to regularly reflect on the documentation. Reflective discussions happen during equity visits, typically at the end of the day; however, it is critical to plan for more extended reflections on the community's learning and practices. These should take place not only among the planning and facilitation team(s) but also within the full

learning community. For example, a meeting might begin with participants individually reviewing the prior month's written reflections, then
discussing implications for future work. Or part of a meeting might be
devoted to a reflection on the previous month's equity visit, informed by
a review of the patterns and wonderings that emerged. While the focus
may be on one district's visit, participants are then encouraged to make
connections to their own equity context and goals, as well as to what the
community is learning about equity and instruction. Reflections also
inform changes in the visit structure and specific protocols that make
them more effective.

DRAWING ON ORGANIZATIONAL TOOLS

In carrying out the planning, facilitation, and documentation roles,
learning communities rely on a range of tools. In the next section, we
describe three core categories of tools: norms, protocols, and templates.
As we note, many of these tools can be found in Appendices C and D.

Establishing Group Norms

Norms represent an agreement among individuals in a group on how
they will work together, interact, and communicate. By making these
expectations explicit, norms create an environment in which relational
trust is more likely to develop. When communities agree to a set of
norms, participants are more comfortable offering and receiving substantive feedback. Doing so fosters reflective practice and a sense of
professional accountability to the group's shared values and commit-
ments, including those related to equity.

For any group planning to conduct equity visits and discussions of
equity and instruction, it is important to develop a set of norms early
on. In our first meeting, NJNS developed norms that specified expectations for active listening, valuing other perspectives, confidentiality,
and even attendance (see Figure 3.2).

The norms served us well for our meetings outside of schools;
however, as we spent more time in classrooms, we realized that we
needed a separate set of norms for behavior and communication within
schools (see Figure 3.3). These norms were especially helpful for new
members who did not have as much experience with the descriptive
and nonjudgmental principles underlying these types of classroom
observations.

Norms are living documents: To be effective they must be regularly
revisited, reflected upon, and revised. This is especially important if a
group's composition shifts and new members join. But even in a group
with stable membership, in which norms become internalized and the
community develops a strong sense of relational trust, it is crucial to

> **Figure 3.2   Meeting Norms for the New Jersey Network of Superintendents**
>
> - Be present and prepared and participate in meetings
> - Active listening
> - Meaningful work with no commiserating
> - Environment conducive to risk taking
> - Stay focused on mission, purpose, growth, and improvement
> - Value each other's voice and opinion
> - Importance of confidentiality
> - Complete honesty
> - Be attentive to patterns of participation
> - Regular attendance is vital to building camaraderie
> - Communication devices used only during breaks (let the group know if you have an issue that makes it problematic to observe this norm)
> - Observe time limits outlined in meeting agendas and check for group consensus before deviating from the schedule

> **Figure 3.3   Classroom Visit Norms for the New Jersey Network of Superintendents**
>
> - We are here to learn, not to pass judgment
> - We are guests in a place that exists for children's learning and should behave at all times accordingly
> - Avoid conferring with colleagues inside classrooms where teaching and learning are taking place
> - Focus on the instructional core—the interaction of teacher and students around content
> - Electronic communication devices must be turned off during equity visits, except during breaks
> - Seek evidence and challenge assumptions
> - Be open to learning from observing classroom practice and from interaction with colleagues

regularly reflect on the norms. Reflection allows the group to recommit to its shared expectations, refine existing norms, and consider new norms. Creating a set of norms is itself a group learning experience, one that benefits from the use of a protocol and a facilitator familiar with the practice of norms. Many protocols exist to support practitioners in setting norms, such as the National School Reform Faculty's (2014) Setting Agreements Activity.

Using Discussion Protocols

During equity visits and other activities within an equity-focused learning community, much of the learning occurs through discussion. As we described above, facilitation plays a key role in supporting discussions that are inclusive and focused. Protocols provide facilitators with tools to ensure that discussions are purposeful and model the principles of a learning community—relational trust, reflective practice, and professional accountability (Blythe, Allen, & Powell, 2015; McDonald, Mohr, Dichter, & McDonald, 2013).

While there are many protocols for different purposes (see Appendix D: Resources for Protocols), all share two core elements: (1) they provide a structure, or set of steps, the group follows, and (2) they specify roles that individuals within the group will play (e.g., facilitator, presenter, timekeeper, participant). These impositions on so-called natural discussion can feel confining or artificial at first, but they serve to keep the group focused on its purpose and to create an inclusive space for all participants to participate actively. Protocols and facilitation can support educational leaders in talking about instruction in ways that are specific and productive, which can be challenging in light of other concerns (Allen, Roegman, & Hatch, 2015).

The balance of structure and inclusion is especially important in discussions that address race, which, as we discuss in Chapter 4, educators commonly sidestep. Conversations about race, Arao and Clemens (2013) maintain, need to change from "safe" spaces, in which no one is made uncomfortable, to "brave spaces," in which diverse opinions are valued and participants are aware that their perspectives might cause discomfort. Instead of aiming to keep everyone safe, conversations about race may involve moments of discomfort that can support participants' learning. Protocols seek to make the purpose and the structure of the discussion clear to participants so that they are prepared to enter into such brave spaces.

The protocols used in equity visits and planning and debrief meetings reflect a range of purposes, from offering one another feedback in developing or refining an identifiable equity focus to reflecting on a just-completed equity visit. For example, an adaptation of the Tuning Protocol, developed by Joseph McDonald (School Reform Initiative, n.d.), typically conducted a few weeks prior to the visit, can support the host leadership team "fine-tune" key elements of an upcoming equity visit. This protocol, which takes about 60–75 minutes, begins with the host team briefly presenting their equity focus, problem of practice, and look-fors (often using PowerPoint slides and/or handouts). Following the presentation, participants ask "clarifying questions," which the presenting team answers as succinctly as possible. The participants then ask "probing questions" intended to challenge the team's assumptions and point to possible gaps, for example, between a team's equity focus or problem of practice and the visit schedule. The discussion using this protocol provides the host team with a range of feedback they can use to shape the visit so that it is more likely to achieve its purposes.

Some of the other protocols used regularly by NJNS are:

- **Learning Together Consultancy Protocol** – Used to provide all participants with feedback on their equity focus (usually in triads, with each leader/team getting about 20–30 minutes to present and receive feedback)

- **Developing Patterns and Wonderings Protocol** – Used during equity visits following classroom observations, interviews, and other data collection activities in order to synthesize a set of patterns and wonderings related to the problem of practice

- **Next Steps Protocol** – Used after reporting out patterns and wonderings during an equity visit to brainstorm next steps for the host leadership team

Each is described in more detail in Chapter 2 and included in Appendix D. Appendix B also includes several resources that support learning communities in using protocols. To help make sure a protocol is serving the community's purpose, it is important to take time to debrief the protocol after its use, for example: What worked? What can we change the next time we use the protocol?

Designing Common Templates

To support individuals' thinking at different points in the work, NJNS uses a range of templates. These are typically graphic organizers or blank tables/charts aligned to a specific purpose that participants complete in advance of or during a meeting. They allow all participants to consider the same questions and bring artifacts and data related to them to share with colleagues and receive feedback on. In particular, we have used templates to help leaders organize and present data related to their equity focus. Using the same templates over time also allows planning and facilitation teams to collect data systematically, which supports documentation and reflection in the ways we discussed above.

In advance of discussions in which participants share their progress on their equity focus, templates provide guidance about what types of information should be shared. NJNS developed an Equity Focus Feedback Template to help hosts prepare for consultancy protocols (see Appendix D); the template prompts participants to create three to five presentation slides responding to these questions: What is your equity focus? What key strategies are you using to address this focus? What data are you collecting to measure progress? What are your next steps? What questions do you have moving forward? The combination of template and protocol has contributed to discussions that are brief yet have provided useful feedback to the participants—and to the community's learning overall about equity and instruction.

As discussed in Chapter 2, every NJNS meeting concludes with a learning journal template (see Appendix C). The template asked participants to respond anonymously to three questions: What worked well? What remains unclear? How can we increase learning in future meetings? This brief activity has given individuals time and structure to reflect and has provided important documentation for the design team to use in shaping future meetings.

BUILDING SUPPORTS FOR EQUITY-FOCUSED LEARNING AND PRACTICE

Whether in-district or cross-district, equity-focused learning communities require attention to planning, facilitation, and documentation in order to develop relational trust, reflective practice, and professional accountability. These three features provide a foundation to support participants in developing their leadership practice related to equity and instruction. Without sustained and job-embedded professional learning, it is too easy for busy administrators to attend only to the immediate day-to-day demands of their jobs. Equity may fall off their to-do list. Participating in an equity-focused learning community enables educational leaders to integrate equity into their daily work with the support, feedback, and guidance of like-minded colleagues. As Superintendent Kniewel reflected on her participation in NJNS: "It was professional learning that was embedded in my day-to-day work with a structure for sustainability, a shared vision, and a common goal."

Equity-focused learning communities break the isolation of leaders and support them in developing their individual leadership practice. In this chapter, we have seen how the features, organizational components, and specific tools of a learning community can foster attention to equity. Making this transformation is never easy. The greatest challenges to doing so often relate to how leaders and educators generally do or do not talk about race. In Chapter 4, we consider how racism perpetuates inequities and how equity-focused leaders take on race and racism explicitly as part of their core leadership role.

CHAPTER FOUR

TALKING ABOUT RACE AND RACISM

Not everything that is faced can be changed, but
nothing can be changed until it is faced.

—James Baldwin, American Novelist,
Playwright, and Social Critic

The majority of people in the United States live relatively racially isolated lives, with few opportunities to talk authentically about race with people of different racial backgrounds (Bonilla-Silva, 2017). This is as true for educational leaders as for anyone else. But when it comes to serving as equity-focused leaders, these individuals need to develop the ability to involve others within their school or district, including teachers, counselors, board members, community members, and other leaders, in addressing and advancing racial equity. This work requires talking about race and racism and their impact on students' educational experiences—a topic that does not regularly arise in leadership preparation (Gooden & Dantley, 2012).

In this chapter, we examine the necessity of explicitly addressing race in the context of equity and instruction—no matter what the district demographics. We consider some of the challenges to making race central to equity-focused leadership, and we offer some lessons and strategies for doing so more effectively.

ACKNOWLEDGING RACE IN PREK–12 SCHOOLS

The need to address race in schooling is well established; educational policies and practices continue to limit opportunities for students of color, with dire consequences for these students' outcomes, from test scores to graduation rates (Carter & Welner, 2013; Noguera, 2003; Skiba, et al., 2011). This is true across school and district contexts. It is the exception, not the rule, to find a school with an equal proportion of students by race scoring proficient on state exams, or to find students of color, particularly Black and Latinx students, overrepresented in honors and advanced coursework. Instead, these students are much more often overrepresented in discipline statistics and in self-contained classes for students with disabilities (Ford, 2011; Skiba, et al., 2008). Black and Latinx youth also make up a disproportionate percentage of students involved in the juvenile justice system, as well as those in the "pipeline" to incarceration. While people of color make up less than half of the population of the United States, they make up about 60% of the total prison population (Sentencing Project, 2017).

Whether a district is 100% students of color or 5% students of color; whether it is in an urban, suburban, or rural environment; whether affluent or poor, recognizing the centrality of race to students' educational experiences is essential to advancing equity.

PARTICIPANT REFLECTION

Standing Alone, Shouting This at the Rooftops

Color-brave leaders, argues Mellody Hobson (2014), willingly engage in authentic and proactive conversations about race. One longtime NJNS superintendent has adopted a "color-brave" approach to leadership within the district. The leader chose to be quoted anonymously in this book, to protect the ongoing work in their district addressing racial inequities in access to Advanced Placement (AP) coursework.

What I am trying to message to my community is this: Don't tell me that because the majority of poor kids are kids of color, that they can't do well. I recently shared data around AP math and science courses with my board and leadership team. I was shocked to find that not a single Hispanic kid was taking an AP math class. That was a real wake-up call for our administrative team and gatekeepers.

In our work going forward, we are developing a Disproportionality Task Force looking at institutional barriers to diversity in AP. We are offering the PSAT during the school day, and we are using that to identify students with AP potential. We are brainstorming different ideas, some of which are very expensive. But at least we are talking about it, and the sky hasn't fall down. I am pleased to say, we have a few Hispanic kids taking AP math next year.

Addressing racial equity is always on my mind. The last thing that I want to do is to acquiesce on race. The network is helpful, knowing that there is a team behind me. Even if I'm standing alone shouting this at the rooftops, there are people standing on other rooftops that I meet with every month. Yeah, my voice is getting a little worn on this, but it's the right work.

Racial disparities in schools manifest themselves in a range of ways. While they are often correlated to students' socioeconomic status, they persist even for students of color from middle class and upper class family backgrounds (Ladson-Billings, 2006; Reardon & Galindo, 2009; Singleton, 2014). Educators' responses to these disparities have often been to blame students of color, their families, and communities for low performance. Going hand in hand with "blaming the victim" are forms of "deficit thinking" common in discussions of students of color and underserved youth. Deficit thinking refers to the idea that something is wrong with students or their families; because of these deficits, students are unable to engage in challenging academic content (Valencia, 2010). It may appear benevolent, such as when educators suggest that they do not want to frustrate students by having expectations for their work that are too high; however, as President George W. Bush (2000) and others have put it, low expectations for underserved students are their own form of bigotry.

Another phenomenon that affects educators' capacity to address the reality of racial disparities in students' educational experiences is the adoption of color-neutral responses to race. Being color-neutral means intentionally avoiding explicit acknowledgment of students' racial backgrounds, racial disparities in student data, or the role of race and racism in society (Bonilla-Silva, 2017). Individuals who adopt a color-neutral stance often believe merely naming race is itself a racist act. Such approaches, even when framed in egalitarian terms, deny the intractable web of beliefs, policies, and practices that have perpetuated racial disparities in public education.

For many educational leaders, it may seem easier to avoid talking about race than to acknowledge that their district's or school's own structures and policies institutionalize and perpetuate racial disparities—and that they can do something about it. Educational leaders ready to confront racial inequities need help in initiating and sustaining conversations about race and racism, ones that have the potential to address, transform, and eliminate inequitable structures, policies, and practices in their schools and districts.

TALKING ABOUT RACE IN PREK–12 SCHOOLS

A growing literature demonstrates that race is a subject that most leaders choose to avoid (Brooks, 2007; López, 2003; Rusch & Horsford, 2009; Tatum, 2007; Young & Laible, 2000). In the face of this reality, the work of equity-focused leaders is to address race explicitly. They do this by leading conversations in their schools and districts that focus on systemic racism and how it impacts students of color. When they hear teachers blame students of color or their families for low performance, equity-focused leaders call out systemic racial inequities that prevent student success.

Even as social justice and equity have become more present as topics in conversations in preK–12 education, race itself has remained largely implicit. It exists, if at all, in the coded language of phrases such as "at-risk," "urban youth," or "underperformance" (Milner, 2012). Our experiences with NJNS and in many other settings have made clear that educational leaders cannot effectively address racial inequities unless students' racialized identities are explicitly named and discussed. For this reason, we have adopted the motto, "If we are not talking about race, we are not talking about race."

Leaders may avoid leading explicit discussions of race for a variety of reasons (Gooden & Dantley, 2012; McMahon, 2007). They may feel unprepared to do so by their leadership preparation program. Their life experiences with people of other races may be limited. They may fear professional repercussions—losing their job, being reassigned, or facing resistance and criticism from their communities. Or they may believe that addressing issues of race is itself a racist practice and that it is better to avoid identifying students' race, thereby adopting a color-neutral approach.

Regardless of where such beliefs might have originated, educational leaders need purposeful and sustained opportunities for professional learning related to race so that they become comfortable talking about race and racial inequities in students' experiences. These include learning opportunities like the equity visits we describe in this book, as well as others such as reading and discussing research studies, case studies, and first-person accounts of race in schools; training in disaggregating data by race (and other key demographics, such as disability or socioeconomic status); and opportunities to learn from practitioners who have initiated work on race in their schools and districts.

As we discussed in Chapter 3, such learning experiences will be more powerful—and more likely to occur—in the context of a professional learning community. Equity visits in particular support individual leaders, and the community as a whole, not only in talking about race when analyzing evidence from classroom observations or interviews, but in leading initiatives and facilitating discussions that explicitly address race and racism.

Before addressing some of the challenges related to initiating explicit conversations about race and some productive ways to anticipate these challenges, we consider how doing so is experienced differently by white leaders and by leaders of color.

DIFFERENT CHALLENGES FOR LEADERS OF COLOR AND FOR WHITE LEADERS

Making race the center of a school or district's work—and keeping it at the center—is challenging for all leaders; however, individual leaders' racial backgrounds create different types of challenges. Leaders of color talking explicitly about race and racism risk being accused by white educators and community members as only interested in helping "their kind"—students (or teachers) who share their heritage (or perceived heritage) (Jones, 2002). For example, a Latinx superintendent or principal may be accused of caring *only* about Latinx students (Ortiz & Ortiz, 1995), while a white leader is unlikely to be critiqued by a school board for caring only about "their kids."

Black leaders raising issues of race and racism in particular risk being identified as "another angry Black person"—even if they are saying or doing the same thing a white, Latinx, or Asian leader might be saying or doing (Wingfield, 2007). Leaders of color may also be assumed by white colleagues to serve as spokespeople for their entire race (Harper et al., 2011), whereas a white person sharing their perspective is rarely, if ever, assumed to be a spokesperson for all white people.

In conversations with white colleagues, participants of color who share personal experiences of racism may wonder how white colleagues will respond or what they will think and say or not say (Sue, Lin, Torino, Capodilupo, & Rivera, 2009). Will they agree that the experience shared was racially motivated? Will they dismiss the pain their colleague experienced? Will they recognize their colleague's vulnerability in sharing it?

White educational leaders face different challenges in talking about race. In simply identifying race as a factor or possible factor, for example, in students' test scores, they may fear being seen as "racist." Instead, consistent with the color-neutral ideology that suggests leaders focus on students as individuals and ignore systemic realities such as racism (DiAngelo, 2011, 2018), white educators may choose not to say anything about race at all. In fact, many white people in the United States have largely been insulated from difficult conversations about race, making them more likely to choose to remain silent. DiAngelo's (2011) concept of white fragility, the "state in which even a minimum amount of racial stress becomes intolerable, triggering a range of defensive moves" (p. 54), explains this type of response by white individuals. When white leaders do take part in conversations about race and racism, they are more likely than leaders of color to experience these conversations as uncomfortable and destabilizing (DiAngelo, 2011, 2018). This is true when race is merely named; greater discomfort comes when white leaders' implicit biases or privilege are called out or challenged by people of color.

Feelings of discomfort are rooted in the social privilege white people have experienced, often unconsciously, in the United States (and other countries). They are compounded by the mostly tacit societal acceptance of white superiority. The result is that white leaders are less likely to tolerate racially stressful discussions. When race does come up explicitly in conversations, white individuals often become defensive, resentful, or even angry (DiAngelo, 2011, 2018).

For equity-focused leaders, no matter their race or the demographics of their school or district, recognizing these challenges is critical to creating conditions to talk explicitly about race and racism. The leader's own willingness and ability to talk about race in explicit, productive ways will significantly influence whether and how others do so—with the potential to impact the educational experiences, opportunities, and outcomes of students. In the remainder of this chapter, we consider some specific challenges to addressing race explicitly, and some strategies for overcoming them.

CHALLENGES TO MAKING RACE CENTRAL TO DISCUSSIONS OF EQUITY IN SCHOOLS

Our work with NJNS, as well as our work with individual schools and districts, has brought us face to face with the challenges that educational leaders commonly face in making race central to taking on inequity in students' educational experiences, opportunities, and outcomes. In the sections that follow we describe four of these: (1) culture of nice, (2) sticking to the protocol no matter what, (3) understanding race, and (4) white silence.

For each, we describe strategies that can be employed to address the challenges and, more generally, initiate and deepen conversations about race and racism within schools and districts. We call these strategies "anticipatory actions," because they allow leaders to both anticipate the kinds of challenges they will face in doing equity work and act in ways that prevent such challenges from negatively affecting the work.

In sharing these challenges and strategies, we recognize that the work is difficult and long-term: Quick fixes do not exist. We are not offering a prescriptive curriculum that, if adopted, would effectively confront and disrupt racism and racial inequity in all schools or districts. Instead, we are speaking from our own experience and speaking our own truth. These are some of *our* answers to the challenges that equity-focused leaders face. Each leader or community of equity-focused leaders will need to find the approaches that work for them in their own contexts.

The challenges themselves are not unique to equity visits. They are endemic to any initiative that explicitly calls out race and racism. When they arise, equity-focused leaders should see them not as obstacles but as opportunities to move the work forward and engage others in the work.

Before taking on the individual challenges, we describe two anticipatory actions that support communities in making race central to equity work: having courageous conversations and providing exemplars of "color-brave" leadership in which leaders willingly initiate and engage in conversations about race.

Anticipatory Action:
Practice Courageous Conversations

Honest discussions about race can occur at any point. However, recognizing that most educators do not have experience participating in or leading such discussions, it is important to be deliberate in creating opportunities for them to do so. Based on challenges within NJNS, described in the following sections, we initiated courageous conversations as a core part of our regular meetings. Drawing on Singleton and Linton's (2006) initial work, which Singleton (2014) has continued to develop, we regularly devote a segment of meetings when we are not conducting an equity visit to an explicit conversation about race and education.

We often use videos and texts that highlight voices of people of color in response to current events. For example, as a community, we viewed individuals from different racial and ethnic groups speak about their experiences in the *New York Times* (2015) video series "A Conversation on Race." In small groups, we then connected what we had heard to our own personal and professional experiences.

In order to engage all participants in discussions about race, it is important that they be facilitated and that everyone commit to a set of norms for these discussions. We adopted the norms outlined by Singleton and Linton (2006): stay engaged, speak your truth, experience discomfort, and expect and accept non-closure. In learning journals completed at the end of meetings and in interviews, participants have reported that these regular opportunities to talk about race within NJNS have supported them in building the skills, knowledge, and relationships needed to initiate conversations about race in their schools and districts.

Anticipatory Action: Provide Exemplars of Color-Brave Leadership

Guest speakers and readings can offer powerful resources for leaders in taking on race and racism. They provide real-life examples of equity-focused practitioners who talk about race intentionally in their own educational contexts. They offer not only inspiration that this type of leadership is possible but also concrete ideas and strategies for those who want to get started but are unsure how to do so.

In NJNS, we have invited superintendents from other districts to share their stories and interact with our community, including the presentations by Weast and Lacey discussed in Chapter 1. We have also asked members of the NJNS community to share from their own life and work. Reading and discussing accounts by equity-focused leaders can also be powerful. For example, Childress, Doyle, and Thomas's (2009) description of Jerry Weast's and Freida Lacey's work in Montgomery County, Maryland, offers clear examples of both their commitment to racial equity and practical suggestions for how to engage in the work.

Challenge: Culture of Nice

One phenomenon that all schools and districts experience is the *culture of nice* (City, Elmore, Fiarman, & Teitel, 2009). The culture of nice, as we introduced in Chapter 1, refers to a professional climate in which individuals refrain from challenging or questioning each other's practice. In a "nice" school, classroom doors are typically closed, and teachers practice in virtual isolation—and bereft of critical feedback—from one another.

It is easy to see how the culture of nice interacts with prevailing color-neutral approaches to inhibit individuals in raising issues of race. In NJNS, from the start we recognized that this culture would be a major impediment to talking about equity—one of our earliest norms for discussion, "complete honesty," anticipated this challenge. Even when called out, the culture of nice remains a constant threat to inquiry and critical reflection in general and, in particular, to examining racial inequities.

In equity visits, examples of nice comments and questions were common even when observers were encouraged to frame probing questions, or "wonderings," related to the evidence they had collected and the host team's problem of practice and equity focus. Observers were far more likely to ask questions that did not explicitly name race. They rarely asked direct questions that could be considered challenges to district practices and beliefs—and thus perceived as challenging a colleague or colleagues.

In place of nice comments, we strive to be direct in our discussions of equity, instruction, and race. Being direct often means challenging the recipient of the comment to take action or justify why actions have not been taken (see Figure 4.1). Being direct in this way requires the relational trust a community works to create and maintain, and it builds that trust.

Anticipatory Action: Establish Norms

Relational trust is crucial for conversations about race, especially among racially diverse participants. However, discussions about race cannot wait until an atmosphere of complete trust exists; thus, these discussions must take place concurrently with developing trust. Courageous conversations like those described above help to build trust, which in turn make it more possible for direct discussions, rather than those that perpetuate the culture of nice. Another effective way to build trust and contribute to more direct feedback is to first recognize the pervasiveness of the culture of nice, then establish norms that intentionally seek to challenge it, for example, a norm of "complete honesty." As important as it is to establish norms, the need to revisit them regularly is equally important—asking "How are we doing in terms of combatting the 'culture of nice'?" (See Chapter 3 for more on developing norms.)

Figure 4.1   Nice vs. Direct Comments

The examples below are based on discussions from NJNS equity visits. In each, we contrast a "nice" comment or observation, which actually was made, with what would be a "direct" way of addressing the same issue.

	Nice Comment	Direct Comment
Example 1	It seemed, when you framed this, you talked about the fact that, if teachers and administrators in the schools were learning and engaging in professional discourse, it would help in practice to support a culture and climate and processes that would help you reduce the achievement gaps, so that somehow these processes. . . .	This initiative is not going to reduce racial achievement gaps.
Example 2	Is there a strategy for helping kids in the classroom? [Note: Yes/No question]	What are the specific strategies you are employing to help students of color?
Example 3	Why are there 6 levels of math at this grade level?	What are you doing to dismantle the levels and get these kids out of low-level academic work?
Example 4	Were any replacement classes for students in special education addressing the same challenging curriculum and standards of performance expected in the regular education instructional program? [Students with certain disabilities took a basic skills literacy class that replaced English 9.]	Why don't you get rid of replacement classes?

Anticipatory Action: Develop Habits of Critical Feedback

Along with relational trust, equity-focused communities are empowered by the feedback participants provide to one another. However, even in discussions that call for critical feedback, the culture of nice is likely to crop up. Participants are often concerned that feedback, like some of the "direct" comments and questions above, will offend the recipient, who is, after all, a colleague. In NJNS, we employ protocols that explicitly call for "cool" as well as "warm" feedback, as well as for intentionally "probing questions." (See Chapter 3 and Appendix D.)

Useful tools, on their own, will not overcome "nice" comments or questions. Facilitators and members of the group must be vigilant in calling out such questions and comments. Often the most effective way to do so is to ask follow-up questions such as, "How does that observation relate to the data we've seen on how Black students are performing in relation to whites?" or "How might race have played a role in that pattern?" Facilitators also help participants to move beyond the culture of nice by modeling more direct comments or questions and probing assumptions that may underlie the comments and questions participants make.

Challenge: Sticking to the Protocol No Matter What

One of the ways individuals and groups may avoid talking about race is by closely adhering to guidelines for discussion or observation (e.g., problem of practice, classroom look-fors) that do not specifically identify race or call for explicit discussion of race. In other words, they stick to the protocol no matter what they observe in classrooms or hear in interviews.

In an early NJNS visit, the network visited Pemberton Township High School, a building with 1,100 students, of whom 50% are white, 35% are Black, and 10% are Latinx. Forty-five percent of the school's students qualify for free- or reduced-price lunch. The problem of practice targeted "engaging students in challenging assignments through student-centered instructional approaches and increased rigor." In the depiction of the discussion below, we underline moments that represent following the protocol no matter what.

Observing groups had just reported out patterns and wonderings, and a facilitator asked school faculty members if they had any questions or comments. After a few seconds of silence, a teacher commented that the school had been more successful in the past, when students were grouped by ability, but now they were all "jumbled together" in heterogeneous classes. She asked if the observers "saw any evidence that heterogeneous grouping was not working."

One of the observers responded, "That wasn't one of our specific look-fors. . . . We saw variations of differentiation, but that wasn't something we focused on." Other observers shared similar perspectives, pointing out that "It's hard for us to know in a 10–12 minute snapshot."

At this point, the facilitator for this discussion intervened, stating, "In respect of this being a Friday afternoon, we're going to leave the continuation of this conversation in the capable hands of the Pemberton staff to engage our thoughts in whatever way you deem appropriate."

This conversation illustrates how the observers' attention to the protocol denied an opportunity to engage with teachers and administrators in a conversation about ability grouping. Most of the observers supported heterogeneous grouping of students. They were aware of research that ability grouping leads to inequitable outcomes for students in the lowest academic levels or groups, who also are predominately Black and Latinx students, students in poverty, and students receiving special education services (Grissom & Redding, 2015; Skiba et al., 2008). In this case, observers used the protocol, that is, the specific focus of the problem of practice, as well as the schedule (i.e., time of day), as rationales for not taking up the teacher's question about ability grouping.

This is not to say that protocols should be discarded as soon as a controversial issue arises. Protocols play an important role in keeping the visit focused and involving all participants in the discussion. And, since the protocol for an equity visit identifies the problem of practice that has been determined by the host school and/or district, it is important that observing teams honor their intended focus in sharing their patterns and wonderings. Doing so, however, should not constrain observers from raising issues of race, or any other potential inequity, that are pertinent to the topic at hand but were not explicitly stated in the problem or look-fors. Allowing that to happen defeats the very purpose of equity visits—shining light on the conditions that maintain inequitable learning opportunities for some students.

Anticipatory Action: Use an On Ramp

Facilitators in equity visits strive to keep the group focused on the equity focus presented by the host, as well as on schedule. They are charged with accomplishing all of the significant parts of the visit, from introduction of the problem through reflections on the day, ending at a predetermined time—for NJNS visits, this has typically been a Friday afternoon. However, facilitators also bear a special responsibility to create conditions for the group to explore issues related to race and racism as they emerge from observing classrooms, interviewing teachers and students, and reviewing other forms of evidence. Often these responsibilities conflict; this is especially true, as in the Pemberton High School visit, when big issues related to equity are raised late in the day, for instance, during a host team's reflections on patterns or wonderings, or even during the final reflections on the visit.

In these situations, it is sometimes possible to discuss an emergent issue—for example, if the group agrees to extend its meeting time to discuss it. However, given the importance and complexity of such issues, it is not always possible to have a full or even partial discussion in the moment. In such case, the group can put the issue or question on its "on ramp" to be discussed at the next meeting. As facilitators, we have seen many important topics put into "parking lots," never to be discussed again. Being placed on the on-ramp, by contrast, should be taken as an imperative for the host team and/or facilitators to determine how and when the issue or question will be discussed, for example, by designating time for exploration in the next meeting and providing an appropriate structure for the discussion.

Anticipatory Action: Modify the Protocol

As we noted, protocols serve important purposes in keeping participants focused and supporting inclusive discussions. However, protocols are meant to help participants investigate inequities, not sidestep them.

For this reason, protocols should always be seen as "living documents," to be modified based on the kinds of critically reflective double-loop learning that occurs within equity-focused learning communities, as described in Chapter 3.

The protocols we include in this book have been revised many times, in response to our community's reflections on the visits and other meetings and in particular on how the protocols serve their purposes within that context. The practice of equity visits itself has been revised, as described in Chapter 1. For example, reflecting on early experiences of focusing on "all students" led us to make equity explicit in the problem of practice and look-fors by having hosts name specific groups of students whose educational experiences, opportunities, and outcomes were inequitable.

Finally, it is important that observers understand that protocols are meant to serve the purposes of investigating issues of equity. The goal is not completion of the protocol or an orderly and well-timed discussion. When an observer sees something on a visit that suggests inequity or racism, they should name it, even if it is just one incident in one classroom. The group, working with its facilitators, needs to figure out how to address it within the visit or at a designated time later on.

Challenge: Understating Race

One of the ways that educators elude taking on issues of race is to understate them. This occurs when leaders use color-neutral language or talk about inequities that impact "all" students, rather than explicitly naming racial groups that are disproportionately affected. Understating race also occurs when leaders look to nonracial explanations, such as poverty or disability, for disparities in opportunity or achievement. The effect, whether consciously intended or not, is to minimize the impact of race and racism through avoiding or rejecting racial considerations.

In NJNS, even when race has been part of the problem of practice, understating race has occurred during equity visits themselves. An example of this took place at an equity visit focused on the academic performance of students of color in middle school language arts classes. During the visit, the look-fors for classroom observations asked observers to pay special attention to how students of color engaged with the lessons.

During the reflections at the end of the day, one of the participants shared a moment that stood out to her:

> . . . one little girl, it really bothered me, an African American girl, she had her hand up, hand up, hand up, and the teacher didn't call on her at all. I was ready to jump out of my skin and go over and say, "Can you please call on this kid?" Now there were a couple of

other kids that raised their hands and weren't called on, but we were focused on the African American students.

Two superintendents shared a possible interpretation of the classroom interaction:

Observer 1: *Even as you talk about a girl who wasn't called on, she may be a Black child who is advanced proficient and the teacher's not calling on her. . . .*

Observer 2: *Because she's calling on her all the time?*

No one countered or challenged the comments made by these observers.

These comments demonstrate one of the ways educators understate the role of race, in this case, by offering alternative reasons that the Black student was not called upon—reasons that have nothing to do with race. Yes, it is possible that the individual student in this case is high performing, as are many Black and Latinx students in this school. It is also possible that she had answered a question or two just before the observers entered the room, and the teacher was now trying to involve other students in the discussion. However, the comments suggest that race is likely to be irrelevant to the interaction and not an issue worthy of discussion. In this instance, they effectively shut down a discussion of race and participation patterns.

In reflecting on this discussion, as design team members, we realized that we had failed in the moment to make this an opportunity for a serious conversation about race and how teachers engage students of different races in discussions and other activities. Such a conversation might have encouraged school and district leaders to develop strategies to use with their teachers for increasing awareness about participation patterns.

Anticipatory Action: Facilitate Vigorously and Vigilantly

Conversations involving race require facilitation that is attuned to both the challenges and opportunities such conversations bring. This begins with the facilitator's awareness of the ways that race may be understated. For example, participants may claim that the interests of "all students" take precedence over attention to students from any single group. Or they may suggest that "a rising tide lifts all boats," in other words, that helping all students will necessarily help the underserved ones too.

Facilitating race-focused discussions also requires awareness of microaggressions that may emerge. Microaggressions are brief and commonplace racial slights that may be made deliberately or unconsciously (Sue et al., 2007). Examples of microaggressions include complimenting Latinx students for how well they speak English or noting how eloquent a Black student is. These types of comments send implicit messages that devalue and insult people who are Latinx and Black. Strong facilitation not only responds to these types of comments but also attends to what is left unsaid. A facilitator might interject, for example, "It is interesting that no one so far has mentioned the race of the students we observed in the resource room . . ." in order to bring the group's attention to a pattern that had not been stated.

Anticipatory Action: Make
Race Explicit in Framing Equity Visits

While no guarantee, it is more likely that observers will discuss issues of race if they are explicitly asked to look for them. In NJNS, design team members work with host leadership teams well before the visit to help frame an equity focus, problem of practice, look-fors, and interview questions that name race. For school communities where it is taboo to discuss race and racism, host leadership teams require support in determining effective ways to make racial inequities a central, explicit part of an equity visit. One strategy is to require hosts to share data disaggregated by race, among other salient demographic characteristics with the observers; for equity visits, hosts also develop an equity focus and problem of practice that name racial inequities.

Challenge: White Silence

In conversations about race in groups with participants of diverse racial backgrounds, white participants often remain silent. This is a common response to feelings of anger, shame, guilt, or hopelessness that many white people experience when talking about race, racism, and the experiences of people of color (DiAngelo, 2011, 2018). White people may fear saying something offensive. They may believe that they have little to contribute because they do not perceive themselves to have had any racialized experiences. Or they may feel that they do not know how to participate. Remaining silent, they believe, may bring them a degree of comfort in an uncomfortable situation.

If they do participate, white participants may opt to "follow the lead" of their colleagues of color. This is how one of the white facilitators in NJNS described his participation in early discussions of race; he looked to Black colleagues to speak up first when an issue of race arose before making a comment of his own—even if he had observed an issue prior to a person of color bringing it up.

Regardless of the reason, when white participants do not speak in conversations about race, this affects everybody involved. Participants of color who take risks by sharing their experiences and perspectives may feel exposed or vulnerable. They may experience frustration and even distrust when white participants do not demonstrate willingness to engage in the conversation (Sue, et al., 2009). White participants who listen but do not share their own experiences or ask thoughtful questions of their colleagues of color sacrifice the opportunity to explore ways that their colleagues experience race and racism in their lives and work. They also miss opportunities for feedback on their own understandings of race. For the group as a whole, opportunities for learning about race and leadership for equity are short-circuited.

At one NJNS meeting, Dr. Edward Fergus, whose research and practice focus on equity and disproportionality, presented strategies that district leaders could use to address racial disparities in schools and districts. The excerpt below comes from the whole-group discussion that followed; it illustrates a rich conversation between leaders of color and a marked silence on the part of white participants—in a group that is majority white:

> **Participant 1, Black woman:** *My district was the color-blind district. As far as I'm concerned, that is not okay. I'm a little less patient with creating change. I've got to be at the forefront of the work. I can't leave it to outsiders.*

> **Participant 2, Black male:** *African American leaders sometimes are perceived to bring a racial agenda, so I have struggled with how to get around that. Another challenge is getting teachers to recognize that they don't have the capacity or belief to successfully teach students of color. I don't know how you get somebody to say, "I really am uncomfortable around Black kids."*

> **Participant 3, Black woman:** *I'm known as the passionate administrator. Being an African American female principal of a predominately white school, I want to bring up issues of race with my school. We have students that are being lost, marginalized. When I do talk about race, the teachers see it as my personal agenda. I am blessed to have two white male vice principals who are willing to lead these conversations for me. And I am saddened that I can't be the spokesperson and lead these conversations, because I have to make everyone else feel comfortable.*

> **Presenter, Latino, Black male:** *That's one of the tensions we have to manage. There are tension points in how we build capacity to understand instructional work along with consideration of how disparities have been manifested over time.*

> **Design team facilitator, Black male:** *I don't know how to ask, but we've had three Black people speak to this and I wonder, what is the tension white people face? What challenges do white*

administrators face in leading these types of conversations? Is there something all of us need to understand?

This pattern of white participants remaining silent in discussions focused on race, called out here by a Black facilitator, was evident in other NJNS conversations. In this case, after the facilitator made this comment, three white participants joined the conversation. Over time, NJNS participants have become more comfortable discussing racial inequities. Still, white participants only rarely share their own personal stories related to race or ask questions of their colleagues of color about their racial experiences.

Anticipatory Action: White Participants Take Responsibility

For an equity-focused community, white silence about race is not tolerable. Nor is it enough to "follow the lead" of colleagues of color. Participants must commit to sharing their perspectives on race, including talking about their own racial identity and asking colleagues of color as well as white colleagues about how race affects their perspectives on education and leadership.

Everybody involved in a conversation about race shares the responsibility for talking openly about race, including talking about their own race. Facilitators, and especially white facilitators, can play an important role in helping other white participants overcome white silence and making themselves vulnerable. This does not mean that they should dominate discussions about race or make the conversations all about themselves; rather, it suggests they should speak up about race and their racial experience rather than relying on colleagues of color to take the lead.

This requires practice and commitment. In NJNS, facilitated courageous conversations about race, like those described earlier in the chapter, have provided opportunities for white participants to gain valuable experience in talking about their own race and learning about others' experiences. Fergus introduced NJNS to role-plays in which participants practice addressing racial microaggressions (see *Solving Disproportionality*, Fergus, 2016); these have helped participants to think about ways to deliberately raise or address issues of race. In the end, white educational leaders need to view their efforts related to racial equity as central to their work, and not something to assign to their colleagues of color.

Anticipatory Action: Identify Patterns of Participation

Taking responsibility begins with awareness. In NJNS, we have periodically shared data, including excerpts from meeting transcripts like the one above, to illustrate discourse patterns within our learning community. This strategy can be applied within individual discussions and meetings, for example, by having a facilitator or designated participant keep track of the number of comments and questions, parsed by race and gender of the speaker, and share these data with the group as part of its reflection. We do not recommend making this a regular practice, but rather one that can be used periodically to initiate critical self-reflection on how the community is doing in terms of talking about race.

KEEPING RACE AT THE CENTER OF THE DISCUSSION

It is all too easy *not* to talk about race. Even among committed equity-oriented leaders, explicit conversations about race may not occur frequently—or at all. As a racially diverse design team, we learned this in dramatic fashion. During a summer retreat, after five years of working together, three of the white team members shared a draft journal article examining some of the ways NJNS participants, including design team members, eluded or curtailed talking about race during equity visits. In their analysis, these three team members identified "racial erasure" as one of the patterns that constrained more sustained explorations of race and equity. Drawn from the work of bell hooks (1992) and applied in education settings by McKenzie and Scheurich (2004), racial erasure occurs when individuals profess to seeing students as race-less (in other words, describe themselves as "color neutral") or when they argue that students' race is not relevant, as exemplified by the example for Understating Race, described earlier in this chapter.

The two Black men on the design team were infuriated that anyone, let alone their design team colleagues, would accuse them of racial erasure. Both have committed their lives' work to confronting racial inequities in school systems across the United States. They pointed to a key difference between how Black and white facilitators experience discussions of race within racially mixed groups. If a white person asks a follow-up question related to race, they are likely to be seen as simply following a protocol that calls for probing questions; if a Black man asked the same question, he is likely be perceived by white participants as being "an angry Black man." White team members had not considered how facilitators' race influenced their practice.

This led to our first truly courageous conversation about race as a design team. The Black design team members pointed out that, from deep experience, they were able to sense when pushing white people to talk about race was likely to push them "away from the table," possibly for good. Thus, what had looked like racial erasure to white colleagues was actually a thoughtful calibration of how to increase the community's focus on race without causing members who were less experienced or comfortable in conversations about race to disengage from the work. For the design team, this conversation was a breakthrough moment in our own capacity to talk about race and racism. It also had impact on our practice of facilitation, as well as on our research and writing. For NJNS, it has led to more explicit and sustained attention to race in equity visits and other network meetings and discussions.

PARTICIPANT REFLECTION

Asking Questions, Avoiding Defensiveness

Superintendent Nancy Gartenberg of Montgomery Township School District described her experiences of racial conversations in NJNS after her second year as a member. As a white woman, she reflects on how the developing relational trust within the group enabled her to engage in conversations about race in ways that supported her work in her district as well as her own learning:

> I recall one time when we wound up having a conversation about the white person's experience with people of color, and the Black perspective on the white person's perspective. I don't think I've ever had such an honest conversation. I think there is a tendency for my white colleagues to feel badly in general for the treatment of Blacks in this country, and there is a Black perspective that the average white person does not get it.
>
> I felt safe—safer, not completely safe in the beginning, because it really was one the first couple of months since I'd been in the network. But there was a sense that people were able to ask a question without somebody being defensive. I think there's an implicit trust in that group for me that what we say in that room doesn't go any further.

As the examples from NJNS in this chapter and book demonstrate, initiating conversations about race and education will surface obstacles of many kinds, including assumptions about students, adherence to inequitable policies, resistance to changing practice, and many others. For the equity-focused leader, bringing these to the surface should be seen as not simply pointing to failure but instead generating the long-term and complex work needed to establish more equitable opportunities and outcomes for all students. Being an equity-focused educational leader means confronting deeply entrenched school and district cultures of silence and avoidance. Changing these cultures, especially within a larger society that perpetuates structural racism, will likely be the greatest challenge of their careers. In Vignette 2, we present the narrative of a conversation about race that happened during an NJNS equity visit, illustrating how participants challenged each other and reflected on each other's perspectives.

While we have focused this chapter specifically on talking about race and racism, a pernicious and long-standing challenge to equity in the United States, we know it is not the only systemic inequity in preK–12 schools in the United States. The challenges and anticipatory actions we have discussed here and the implications we raise in the chapter to come can also be applied to challenges experienced by different cultural and demographic groups, such as students living in poverty and homeless students, LGTBQ students, students with disabilities, and students learning English as an additional language.

VIGNETTE 2

A Conversation About Race and Instruction

In this chapter we have discussed several of the challenges that arise in talking about race, as well as some strategies for addressing them. We now share an actual conversation about race that occurred during an NJNS equity visit. This story is intended to show how an equity-focused learning community can create space for individuals to share strong sentiments related to race and to challenge each other. It also illustrates how individuals and the group draw on what they learned from the experience to reflect on their own practice. In the conversation, we identify moments where courage was called upon to challenge colleagues in relation to issues of race and also to be challenged by colleagues. We keep the participants anonymous, as this conversation adhered to a set of norms that included both an "environment conductive to risk taking" and the "importance of confidentiality" (see Chapter 3).

The Background: An Equity Visit Examining Tracking

The conversation at the heart of this narrative was the culmination of a daylong inquiry into racial patterns in a high school's tracked classes. Students could be placed in one of four levels of Algebra 1, for example, based on their prior year's state assessment scores. The top quartile were placed in the top level, and so on, with the bottom quartile in the lowest level. This equity visit grew out of several years of concern on the part of the superintendent and central office administrators about the persistence of tracking at the high school.

The superintendent, Paul, an experienced leader of color, determined that he had to act. He could no longer wait for community or educator readiness. The racial inequities were glaring—and the U.S. Office of Civil Rights concurred, having just cited the district in relation to race. While the school was about 25% Latinx, 25% Black, and 50% white, white students were most likely to be in the higher tracks (i.e., honors, AP), while Black and Latinx students filled the majority of the seats in the lower tracks.

Superintendent Paul and several administrators held a strong belief that tracking was inherently inequitable. The equity focus they developed examined ways to increase access to higher-track courses for students of color. These courses, he argued, should more accurately reflect the diversity of the student body.

When Paul and his leadership team presented the equity focus to NJNS, they framed the visit around their interest in improving access of Black and Latinx students to higher-track classes. The problem of practice and look-fors they shared with the district staff, however, focused on how the district could better support teachers in adopting instructional strategies that would support diverse students. The look-fors guided observers to focus on teacher questioning and routines, students' participation and assessment of their own learning, and choice of learning resources—none specifically named race; nor did the problem of practice.

During the observation time, observers visited classrooms of different tracks (i.e., all four levels of Algebra 1) and used the look-fors to guide their observations. The observers also quickly noted that higher-level courses enrolled few Black or Latinx students, and lower-level courses enrolled higher numbers of Black or Latinx students. While not specified by the look-fors, the evidence of this disproportionality could not be ignored.

During student interviews, observers met with white, Latinx, and Black students in mixed groups and asked them about their teachers' expectations for them, level of challenge of their courses, and the course selection process. While none of the provided interview questions focused on race, observers asked follow-up questions related to tracking that led several students to comment on their racialized experiences in school. One Black student, for example, noted that even though he had an A in his previous language arts class, his teacher had not recommended him for AP English Language and Composition. He told the group that his parents had to come down to the school to meet with the guidance counselor before he could enroll in the course.

After analyzing evidence from classroom observations and interviews, the small groups shared a number of probing questions:

- Why are there so many tracks [of each subject], and does that aggravate racial patterns?
- How are teachers getting professional development for culturally responsive pedagogy?
- What could students and teachers learn from shadowing students from different tracks?
- Is there an explicit pathway that either limits or increases access of Black and Latinx students to the more challenging academic classes?

One group ended their report with *#TrackThreeIsWhatItShouldBe*, suggesting the district eliminate, at the least, the two lowest tracks for each course, tracks in which very few students passed the state assessment, and in which the majority of students were Black and Latinx.

In-the-Moment Reflections: Was It Racism?

In a brief fishbowl discussion led by the superintendent that followed, district administrators reflected on some teachers' bias, scheduling barriers, and the need for teacher professional development. At times, the reflections became more personal, as different administrators reflected on their own racial identities and how race was impacting students in their building. Aaron, a Black assistant superintendent, declared,

> I am angry. The network is correct that a lot of our children feel these things are racially motivated. I'm angry because it is not going to change. You can't change teachers' mind-sets until people know their own mindset. People here don't think they're racist. I'm really frustrated. We know which classrooms, which teachers, by name, are engaged in racist practice.

His superintendent, Paul, and others acknowledged the truth of what he had said about the racist attitudes and practices of some teachers.

At the end of the day, with only the superintendent and assistant superintendent from the host district present, NJNS participants reflected on the visit. Several issues emerged, including the pace needed for change. Network members also questioned whether the racial patterns they observed in classrooms were a result of systemic racialized district policies and practices. These are charged questions in many schools across the United States, and even among a group of equity-focused educational leaders, different perspectives on them were voiced. The discussion grew heated at times as participants considered how race affected the educational experiences of the students whose classes were observed.

During the discussion, Nathan, a white superintendent from a suburban district with similar concerns about students of color not taking advanced courses, identified his three takeaways and lingering questions about structural issues and teachers' expectations for different groups of students:

> The superintendent had created an environment where staff felt comfortable sharing. In particular, Aaron's [the assistant superintendent] frustration, it sounds like he was feeling that he doesn't have tools to remove a problematic teacher. The second issue, though, is the structure itself, with all the tracking, which leads to the lowering of expectations. The third part, as I see it, is that there may be teachers who are there with you, ready to go. How are you leveraging that?

Notably, he pointed out the untapped potential of those teachers and central office administrators who may already feel a sense of urgency about the racial inequities.

Linda, a Black participant who has worked in a similarly racially diverse district, noted that "students are very tuned in to how this is affecting them. It would be a great opportunity to have the voices of students around the table when the district is having conversations about equity. Students know. They live it every day."

Keith, a white superintendent from a predominantly white district, echoed sentiments shared in the fishbowl by Aaron about the existence of racist teachers who should be let go. "Sometimes in education," Keith said, "we play to the lowest common denominator and allow teachers to just get by. But sometimes, folks need to be hit over the head and be told that they are not doing the job." Referring to teachers who have low expectations for Black and Latinx students, Keith told the host, "People in the building who are 'toxic' need to be singled out and approached in a different way."

(Continued)

(Continued)

Denny, a white design team member, questioned the design of the equity visit, pointing out that it did not explicitly name race as its focus:

> During this visit, it seems like race moved from subtext to text. We saw this in our findings, and we heard it in the district fishbowl, but it wasn't explicit in look-fors. I'm wondering how race ended up at the center since we weren't asked to look for it specifically. I'm wondering how we can build on this experience to make race more explicitly part of the text.

Harry, also a white superintendent, argued that even though race was not in the look-fors, it was central to how the host had framed the visit: "Race was an immediate wondering in our heads before we observed classrooms." He asked, "As a network, do we need specific look-fors around race?"

Caleb, a Black superintendent from a district with mostly students of color, pushed back against the idea that race should override the stated objectives for the visit: "The superintendent invited us to his house, his district. And my small group, we talked *less* about patterns related to the look-fors and *more* about race, expectations, and tracks." He wondered if that is what the host had wanted to happen, or if, in focusing on race and tracks, NJNS refocused the equity visit on something that may have been less useful for the district. Caleb added that talking about "race isn't necessarily something comfortable," and that the network should be attentive to what might happen if it raises issues of race in a district not ready to discuss them.

Tandy, a white superintendent from an affluent suburban district, commented: "Focusing on curriculum without doing work on mindset and cultural competence related to race—you can't have one without the other. That's why the work is so hard." At the same time, she congratulated Paul for the work he is doing, recognizing the difficulty of convincing people who have been committed to tracking to detrack. "You have to celebrate in bits and pieces."

This led to a passionate response by Rodney, a Black former superintendent and a design team member:

> After 400 years of being Black in America and celebrating small bits and pieces, when I heard the district talk about a decade-long plan, I argue that this work has to be taken care of today. I'm sorry, but I can't celebrate minor gains anymore as a Black man. These disparities in our society, they've become fresh wounds. The assistant superintendent, also a Black man, his anger and pain and impatience, that isn't foreign for me. I don't know where I'm going in terms of suggesting an action plan, except that I know that a little bit is not enough. Structural racism penetrates every vestige of our society, particularly our schools, and it needs to be slayed sooner and more systemically than we are thinking about and talking about as a nation and right here in this room.

Bart, a Black man who has worked in similar districts with powerful white constituents, brought the question back to teachers. He linked work on instructional capacity with some teachers' attitudes about race.

I agree with what has been said, the district has two issues. One is capacity: Your people don't understand the work around rigorous student learning. The other is resistance: A percentage of your teachers is responsible for so much of the practice that is bad for kids of color, and it costs you.

Bart suggested that, as Keith had argued earlier, "If we have to go after those teachers, we go after them."

After a brief discussion of a new state law related to terminating teachers, Keith suggested reframing the issue, not as something wrong with individual teachers, but as something wrong with the system itself: "I think we're arguing over a faulty premise. You have a huge structural issue. Generic instructional frameworks are not going to fix it. What high school, other than this one, anywhere in the United States, has so many tracks in any content area?"

Caleb asked, "Didn't we get information that white kids were put in a higher track even if they had the same assessment scores as Black or Hispanic kids? That's not structure; that's institutional racism. If I'm telling the white kid, you can go up, while I'm telling the Black kid, the Hispanic kid, you should stay."

Keith maintained his interpretation, arguing that "You get rid of the tracking because it is racist, but the structure allows it to fester."

Caleb countered, "That *is* racism. There is no BS around that. That's what it is, and we need to call it that."

At this moment, at the end of a long and intense equity visit, the design team member facilitating the reflections noted the time of day and suggested the network consider the best way to continue this important question of racism and structure in student course placements.

Reflections Beyond the Visit: Being Pushed and Putting Down Our Masks

During this equity visit, superintendents raised issues of race that the look-fors and problem of practice had not specified. They challenged the host superintendent on how he was dealing with teachers who held low expectations of students of color. And they challenged each other on whether the pace of change was sufficient and whether the tracking structures were tantamount to racism. In later discussions, as well as in individual interviews, NJNS participants identified the conversations held during this equity visit as evidence of the network's progress and their own personal progress in talking about race. The comments below come from year-end interviews conducted about four months after the equity visit.

Tandy, who had suggested a slow pace might be needed given the amount of work expected of teachers, reflected,

I was okay with the pushback. I say that with a little bit of hesitancy because sometimes I'm not sure if people understood what I was trying to convey, if it was interpreted as "Well we shouldn't have to push people to go so fast." That was clearly not my intent. I understand the pushback—we've waited 200 years and there are so many challenges within society. We have to address belief systems, particularly with our staff, because we want them to believe only the best about what kids can do. But at the same time our schools are only one mechanism to address what is happening in society.

(Continued)

(Continued)

While Tandy was not convinced by Rodney's argument and thought perhaps she had been misunderstood, she acknowledged the legitimacy of his ideas as she continued to think about how she was going to address teacher beliefs within her district.

Caleb and Keith, who had debated whether the issue was one of structure or racism—or the intersection of the two—both found the visit to be significant. Caleb commented: "I thought visiting that district was really important. It reminded me how, unfortunately, race continues to be a factor in people's minds, and it influences how they talk to kids and advise kids." Almost as an aside, he noted that "the debate we had at the end of the meeting, the equity visit, continues to inspire me and challenge me." Keith reflected,

> I pushed the host superintendent real hard, and Caleb got on me. He was upset with what I had said about structures and race. But it was done in a positive way. We were having a conversation. . . . I think people put down all their masks completely and had a conversation about how much work has to be done. That was a powerful day.

Harry, who had participated briefly in the conversation, felt "an energy in the conversation around addressing" the issues identified by the district. "While I was upset with what I saw [during the classroom observations and interviews] and fired up by it, I also enjoyed seeing the fire in the room. I liked watching the discourse, within the network and even within the host district."

Paul, who was challenged to take action to confront teachers' expectations, reflected on his experience as the host:

> The visit to the district was probably the most powerful experience I've had in any professional learning opportunity. It was a brutally honest experience. There were no efforts to sugarcoat anything at any point. It wound up not only dealing with issues that are so prevalent today, but [it also] got underneath some issues that in other places might not be so evident, but are just as real.

A CONTINUING CONVERSATION

In this conversation at the end of an NJNS equity visit, educational leaders of color and those who are white talked about race, challenged each other, and connected their observations to their own practice. While the leaders agreed that the tracking they observed at the high school was inequitable, the conversation illustrates different perspectives on the pace of needed change and the root causes of the tracking—structure or racism. It demonstrates that NJNS participants have developed a degree of relational trust—when they challenge each other, they do their best to stay engaged, clarify or refine their ideas, and consider alternative viewpoints.

The conversation did not resolve the important issues raised during the visit—nor should it be expected to, given our understandings of courageous conversations. As the interviews suggest, participants were still thinking about the ideas raised in the discussion months later, and making connections to their own district contexts.

Such conversations do not take place in isolation. As we discuss in Chapter 3, they require a community that values and promotes professional accountability. Equity visits, in which leaders invite one another into their buildings and classrooms and reflect together on problems of practice related to race and other differences, provide one approach to developing such accountability and fostering such conversations. None of the participants left NJNS because of this interaction, and the network has continued to look for ways to put race at the center of discussions of equity and instruction.

CHAPTER FIVE

LESSONS FOR LEADERS READY TO INTEGRATE EQUITY AND INSTRUCTION

If you don't like the way the world is, you change it. You have an obligation to change it. You just do it one step at a time.

—Marion Wright Edelman,
American Activist for the Rights of
Children and Founder of the
Children's Defense Fund

We began this book recognizing that educational leaders face two daunting challenges: (1) providing high-quality instruction for all students and (2) ensuring that instruction is equitable, in particular for students of color, students in poverty, students receiving special education services, and students learning English as an additional language. The equity visits we describe in earlier chapters provide one approach to integrating educational leaders' work in these two areas.

In this chapter, we reflect on what we have learned through the development of equity visits. We share some of the implications for using equity visits and related practices in schools, districts, and professional networks. We outline implications for individual leaders first, and then broader implications for organizational culture, leadership preparation, and leadership professional development.

IMPLICATIONS FOR INDIVIDUALS

Perhaps the most important lesson we have learned from superintendents, leadership team members, and principals engaged in equity-focused practices is the necessity to make equity a priority. Leaders who make equity an explicit, sustained focus of their leadership practice positively affect the educational opportunities and outcomes for students, especially students of color and other undeserved groups. Equity visits offer leaders one set of tools to make equity central to their leadership. However, conducted in isolation from the leader's day-to-day work, equity visits are unlikely to affect students' experiences.

Rather than viewing equity visits as another item on a checklist, equity-focused leaders make a continuous commitment to involve others in dialogue and reflection on how to advance equity for all students in all classrooms. Equity visits are one component of a systemic equity focus that engages administrators, teachers, students, and communities. What follows are some implications of such a commitment for individual leaders who commit to identify and address systemic inequities in their own school and district contexts.

Examine Your Own Beliefs

Becoming an effective equity-focused leader means first examining your own beliefs about equity and your life experiences related to equity and race. This may be difficult to do on your own—just one of the reasons we have argued that leaders participate in a learning community focused on equity. NJNS member Jared Rumage moved from the principalship of a school that was predominantly Asian, white, and wealthy, to the superintendency of Red Bank Borough Public Schools, a district that is predominantly Latinx and poor. This transition required him to reexamine his beliefs and understanding of inequity.

> *I was still relying on some of my old experiences in my old district, which didn't always relate to my new surroundings and the challenges that we face here in Red Bank. The network enabled me to think about where I am coming from and where I am now.*

Leaders who reflect on their prior professional and personal experiences and beliefs position themselves to understand who they are and what they need to do to lead in different educational contexts.

Whatever their school or district context, leaders benefit from opportunities to reflect on their personal experiences in schools, as well as on their beliefs about race, privilege, and education. Michael Gorman, a founding member of NJNS, retired as superintendent of Pemberton Township Schools in 2015; he reflected on his own identity as a white male and how that affected his leadership of the racially diverse rural district:

> *The issue of white male privilege was very revealing to me. I hadn't thought of myself in that regard and I hadn't really been looking at the advantages I gleaned as a result of it. Reflecting on this privilege affirmed my previous inclination that I am not walking in the shoes of a person of color, and I don't truly understand the issues they face. . . . I can be sympathetic. I can try to be empathetic, but I can't really know what it's like for somebody who is a Hispanic male in this society, or a female.*

Superintendent Gorman attributed his better understanding of equity issues in his own district to his participation in NJNS discussions and to his reflections on them afterward. He recalled one incident in particular that he had initially described to network colleagues as "an issue of discipline," but came to realize it was actually an "issue of race."

Individually or in groups, leaders critically reflect on their beliefs about equity and race—and their relationship to instruction—and consider how their beliefs inform their leadership practice. Without critical self-reflection, school and district leaders risk reproducing inequitable structures and policies.

Create an Equity-Focused Community

As individuals begin to reflect on their beliefs and experiences about equity, it is essential to seek out support from other equity-oriented educational leaders. Together, they can take part in activities that support them to challenge beliefs and ingrained practices in their own schools and districts. It is within the context of such a learning community, described in Chapter 3, that an individual leader will learn about intersections of equity and instruction, develop strategies for confronting inequities, and receive critical feedback to refine (or reconsider) these strategies. The community provides a degree of accountability for continuing the work, especially when few external demands or incentives encourage leaders to address educational equity as a part of their leadership practice.

PARTICIPANT REFLECTION

Stretching My Wings

For Superintendent Tami Crader, NJNS provided her with the knowledge and skills—as well as the peer support—she needed to leave a homogenous, high-performing district and take on a more diverse district facing greater challenges. When she became superintendent of Neptune Public Schools, she quickly identified organizational structures and beliefs that were negatively influencing college and career opportunities for students in poverty and students of color.

> I had learned so much about equity in the network and from superintendents who lead urban districts. I started to look at everything differently. I started to look at student achievement differently, gender issues differently, race differently. I began looking at data

(Continued)

(Continued)

through the lens of equity and diversity, and so I decided that my next position would be in a district that was larger, with more student diversity. I was inspired by my new colleagues in the network to do the work.

If you've been in the field of educational leadership as long as I have been, you need something that forces you to stretch, and to think, and to share ideas, and to hear others' ideas. I decided to stretch my wings.

As I began working in Neptune, I realized there are still many ways that I need to develop in terms of my ability to lead. I can identify if a group is overrepresented in a specific program. And now I am working on questions of why those overrepresentations exist and how can we combat them.

Become an Equity Warrior

Educational leaders who want to lead for equity make a commitment to keeping equity front and center in their work. They make it clear to their staff and community that every single student deserves equitable experiences and opportunities—and that outcomes should not correlate to students' race, class, neighborhood, or any other demographic characteristic.

Being an equity warrior means identifying inequities both within a system and also between systems. For Superintendent Pablo Muñoz of Passaic Public Schools, a district in which almost all students are economically disadvantaged and over 90% are Latinx, thinking about equity begins with "excellence for all." He identified an equity goal of ensuring that all students graduate with at least 15 college credits (primarily through dual enrollment courses or AP exams), a career certification, or both. This goal grew from his recognition that, historically, students in Passaic have had less access to a rigorous education than students from wealthier districts across the state.

In Superintendent Muñoz's definition of equity, it is not sufficient for Passaic students to score proficient on state exams—it is the goal of the district to prepare students for their lives beyond high school. This drives his decision making all the way down to preschool, ensuring that every student meets benchmarks along the path to college and career success. "It takes time to build out the capacity of teachers and the capacity of students to handle the rigor of the course work," Superintendent Muñoz noted. "But once it's built out, then it becomes a part of quality teaching and learning in Passaic."

Equity warriors are aware of the risks of taking on this stance. They are attentive to context, culture, and politics, to school boards and teachers' unions, as they develop systems-wide initiatives targeting long-standing inequities. Even in the writing of this book, several educational leaders who are committed equity warriors chose to remain anonymous so as to not draw attention to—and possibly derail—work under way that is challenging the status quo in their districts.

One such superintendent initiated district-wide conversations on race, class, and students' experiences. The conversations generated "a lot of excitement and unanswered questions and wonderings about where we go." But they also challenged the district's culture, according to the superintendent, in which students, families, and school personnel "have been really good at getting along without actually talking to each other. We don't understand each other." The superintendent identified the work of bringing people together as "my path as an equity-focused leader," one that will ideally bring racially and socioeconomically diverse communities together. The superintendent made it clear that conversations about race and class matter, while also acknowledging the risks that having conversations on racial equity may entail.

IMPLICATIONS FOR SCHOOL AND DISTRICTS AS ORGANIZATIONS

Equity-focused leadership requires commitment to the individual's own learning and actions. It also requires attention to the leader's school or district culture—the often unstated norms, assumptions, and ways of doing things within any organization (Leithwood & Jantzi, 2000). "The role of any leader is to shape the culture of the organization," noted Superintendent Marcia Lyles. Creating a cultural shift requires leaders to understand how the beliefs and norms of the existing culture perpetuate inequity—and actively confront them. Equity-focused leaders work to identify and eliminate inequitable practices and policies, and institute ones that provide all students the opportunities and supports they need to succeed.

Understand an Organization's Existing Cultural Norms and Beliefs

Changing culture begins with understanding current realities. Equity visits and the related practices described in this book provide leaders with tools to investigate the norms, beliefs, practices, and policies that contribute to inequitable opportunities and outcomes for underserved students. In identifying an equity focus for a visit, leadership teams gather and analyze a variety of data. These data will likely include standardized test scores, graduation and referral rates, disciplinary infractions, and other metrics commonly used in preK–12 schools. Equally important are data sets such as climate surveys, classroom walk-throughs, samples of student and teacher work, and conversations with a wide range of stakeholders—students, teachers, counselors, parents, administrators, board members, and others. In one early equity visit, observers reviewing student work samples from two elementary schools noted that the expectations expressed in the feedback teachers offered on students' work were different for each school. Using multiple and different types of data contributes to understanding the prevailing norms and beliefs about students' learning and their capacity to learn.

By combining classroom observations with interviews, equity visits offer powerful opportunities for educators to reflect critically on how norms and beliefs affect students' educational experiences. However, equity visits typically occur only a few times a year. Equity-focused leaders recognize that collecting and analyzing data related to norms, beliefs, access, and outcomes is part of their ongoing work, not just a one-day event. Other measures, such as regular classroom walk-throughs; focus groups with students or even informal conversations with students in the cafeteria; annual teacher, parent, and student climate surveys; and professional learning communities all support leaders in developing a finer-grained understanding of their organizational cultures.

When Laurie W. Newell took on her first superintendency, of the Essex Regional Educational Services Commission (ERESC), she had no prior experience in a county-based school district. The equity issues at ERESC were unique due to the student population—the students were predominantly Black and Latinx, economically disadvantaged, and receiving either special education or alternative education services. Superintendent Newell recognized that she would first need to understand the district context and not just make "change for change's sake." This included getting to know the teaching staff's beliefs about the students they served, as well as students' understandings of why they were there and their goals. While the "foundation was already there from the work of the previous superintendent, Dr. Young [an NJNS member until her retirement]," understanding the context before making any changes would enable her to develop a strategy that would continue to move the work forward.

Implement Evidence-Based Equity Practices and Policies

Reflections and conversations about equity do not, on their own, change cultures; educational leaders must link them to practices and policies that dismantle inequities. As we described in Chapter 3, Superintendent Lyles recognized that in Jersey City Public Schools, almost all stakeholders avoided talking about race, and color-neutral thinking prevailed. She introduced practices that highlighted race as an issue to address explicitly. These involved principals participating in equity visits and sharing their own racial autobiographies. Superintendent Lyles also implemented professional development related to culturally responsive teaching and required data to be disaggregated and analyzed by race, as well as other categories.

As in Jersey City, investigating how data are used provides rich opportunities for understanding and changing the culture and practices of a school or district. Through analyzing data, educators realize that reality may not support their assumptions. Teachers may believe, for example, that economically disadvantaged students are not performing well because they have poor attendance; examining attendance data might show them that this group of students actually has high attendance, and the challenges lie elsewhere, for example in the types of instruction they receive.

PARTICIPANT REFLECTION

Focusing on the Levers That Shift Culture

For many first-year superintendents, surviving each new day feels like a large enough goal. When Jeffrey Moore came to Hunterdon Central Regional High School District, he was determined to do more than survive. He knew that examining disaggregated data could make inequities visible and create a sense of urgency about the need for change among administrators and teachers. From his work as curriculum director of Freehold Regional High School District, Superintendent Moore knew that a key aspect of data analysis was identifying students who "decelerated"—students who moved from more rigorous to less rigorous courses over time.

> I started working with my leadership team in Hunterdon based on what we did in Freehold in terms of having the team think about how we identify equity and what different metrics we might want to consider. How do we measure access and success? My leadership team and I wanted to identify metrics to serve as needles on gauges that we could then rally folks around to take action—without having to do regression analysis or advanced statistics.
>
> I introduced the idea of deceleration in mathematics. As a team, we looked at the traditional college-bound math track, which seemed to be the only math track that anybody talks about, and we saw that it was not working for kids who were not planning on taking calculus. So we are now working to introduce alternatives to calculus that are still rigorous, such as statistics or computer science. I want to broaden the conversation here in Hunterdon County about options and opportunity in mathematics.
>
> The network and Superintendent Sampson's [of Freehold Regional School District] mentoring of me were both crucial to my focus on those sorts of things as levers to shift culture around mathematics and rigor. In high-performing districts, test scores can represent too broad of a brush for painting a picture of access and equity. When you spend so much time with test averages, it can become ingrained in culture to say that everything is going well. It takes focus and effort to get into the data with your staff and move folks along to unpacking that, disaggregating that, asking questions, and zeroing in on the question of, "Are we offering the opportunity to all kids that we say we are offering?"

Connect Equity Visits to Other Strategies

Equity visits, racial autobiographies, explicit conversations about race, disaggregated data analysis, and other practices will not thrive when disconnected from a district's strategic plan or mission. Equity-focused leaders find ways to connect equity visits and other practices to organizational goals and strategies. One key area for integrating equity visits with other work is through the professional development opportunities that leaders design, provide, or facilitate. Leaders can require that teachers or principals make equity an explicit part of their individual professional growth plans. Such plans are often part of a state mandate, with local flexibility around their design and implementation. As Superintendent Lyles in Jersey City and Superintendent Schiff in Hillsborough did, district leaders can organize an equity visit rotation among schools, including planning and debriefing meetings and other opportunities to reflect on how leaders are integrating equity and instruction.

Professional learning communities (PLCs) can expand their focus to incorporate issues of equity. For the PLCs under way in Elizabeth Public Schools, Superintendent Olga Hugelmeyer and her leadership team have identified articles on equity and instruction for teachers and administrators to read and discuss. In addition to the PLCs, teacher leaders and administrators in Elizabeth participate in faculty networks that conduct "data dives"—in-depth examinations of grade-, school-, or district-level data related to one of the district's focus areas. Hugelmeyer described one faculty network's data dive into Algebra 1:

> We went through the data dive process together with the principals. We had a healthy conversation with regard to where we are, what are the expectations, why are we getting the results we are getting. We did a root-cause analysis [see Fergus, 2016]. Then the principals brought our findings back to their schools, sat in their PLC meetings, and had conversations about the data.

Incorporating equity-focused practices into preexisting structures, as Superintendent Hugelmeyer demonstrated, lets educators know that equity is central to their work, not something external to it.

Make a Long-Term Commitment

Addressing systemic inequities is a long-term commitment; it will not be accomplished with a one-stop professional development session or a single equity visit. Superintendent Hayes of Scotch Plains-Fanwood reflected on shifts in her administrative team's culture over time. Hayes, a founding NJNS member, has focused her team on providing equal access to curriculum, especially for Black students and students receiving special education services. In the early years of this work, whenever her administrative team discussed an initiative or a program, she asked about its potential or actual impact on students from these two groups. Over time, she reports, "filtering all initiatives through an equity lens has changed the culture of the district."

Hayes described how teachers and leaders in the district's gifted and talented program questioned how to make this population mirror the overall student population. As a team, they developed a plan to bring in an external consultant to help address ways to increase racial diversity in the program. Then they worked with central office leadership to make the plan a reality. The expectation to consider racial disproportionality had become part of the way they thought about their work.

In the South Orange and Maplewood School District, work on equity has played out over the tenure of three superintendents, all NJNS members at various times in their careers. First, amid heated public debate and a citation from the Office of Civil Rights, then-Superintendent Brian Osborne eliminated tracking at the middle school. His successor, John Ramos, focused on addressing racial disproportionality in access to advanced coursework at the high school level. As part of this focus, he and his administrative team hosted an equity visit to one of the district's high schools. Their problem of practice focused on educators' expectations for Black students.

The long-term work on equity across various superintendents continued when Interim Superintendent Thomas Ficarra took over. He advanced the movement toward equity by eliminating lower levels of mathematics and science courses, which had been populated disproportionately with Black students. Previously, for example, multiple levels of Algebra 1 existed, to which students were assigned based on their eighth grade test scores. Currently, there is only one Algebra 1 course offered to all students who take Algebra in 9th grade. Ficarra noted the importance of continuity in his equity work in the district:

> When I got to the district, the conversation was about excessive leveling [tracking] at the high school. They have been kicking the idea around for 20 years. The equity visit held the previous year, with the previous superintendent, was a big part of the conversation. I took a look and saw the levels were quite excessive. Having been a superintendent in a similar district, I knew we could get rid of levels.

Aware of the resistance the previous superintendents had faced, Superintendent Ficarra was "prepared for a major battle" with the community. Instead, he reported, there was "limited pushback" to the reduction of 15 course levels in mathematics and science. While a range of factors contributed to this outcome—superintendents, sociocultural factors, parents, and so on—this story illustrates that equity-focused change must be sustained over time, usually over years rather than months. Equity-focused change requires continuous, concerted effort. Without it, some Black students in South Orange and Maplewood would still be taking low-level Algebra and Geometry courses from which no students achieved even the proficient level on state exams.

IMPLICATIONS FOR LEADERSHIP PREPARATION AND PROFESSIONAL DEVELOPMENT

School districts, professional development networks, and university partnerships all serve as potential sites for developing equity-focused leaders. Some districts are building their own "principal pipelines" to create a larger pool of strong applicants, identifying potential administrators and providing opportunities to develop the knowledge and skills needed to be successful within the district (Turnbull, Riley, Arcaira, Anderson, & MacFarlane, 2013). However, unless equity is at the center of the programs' goals and practices, they are unlikely to stimulate more equity-focused leadership practices in schools and districts.

Similarly, equity and social justice have been the hallmarks of several leadership preparation programs in the United States for several decades (e.g., Blackmore, 2009; Hawley & James, 2010; Jean-Marie, Normore, & Brooks, 2009). However, even within programs committed to changing existing structures and practices, leadership students and faculty find it challenging to talk about race in meaningful and productive ways (e.g., Carpenter & Diem, 2013; Hernandez & Marshall, 2009). The reality is that school and district leadership preparation programs often fail to prepare leaders adequately to navigate discussions of race and racial disparities.

School districts and preparation programs can work together to support the development of leaders equipped to lead for equitable outcomes for all students. In the following sections, we share some ways professional development providers, university faculty, and others who work with educational leaders can foster equity-focused leadership practices in a range of district contexts. Whatever the context, leadership candidates and educational leaders benefit from learning experiences that allow them to develop and practice the knowledge and skills required to identify and address systemic inequities.

Involve Leadership Teams in Equity-Focused Professional Development

Throughout this book, we have offered images of how districts and schools can nurture leadership development committed to equity and instruction. NJNS superintendents have identified principals and central office administrators to work with them in planning and hosting equity visits, and they often attend network meetings as a team. Several NJNS superintendents have mentored administrators whom they hoped to prepare as future superintendents themselves. In addition to Superintendent Moore, two other former leadership team members from NJNS districts have become superintendents, with more likely to follow. Participating in collaborative learning opportunities across hierarchical levels allows administrators to come to know each other as learners committed to equity, open to learning from and with each other.

Involving leadership team members in equity-focused professional development, like that offered by NJNS and within several member districts, also creates a critical mass for equity work. Superintendent Sampson has frequently brought his curriculum director, chief academic officer, and director of curriculum and instruction to meetings. As a team, they have used these opportunities to develop equity-focused data analysis related to deceleration (described earlier in this chapter).

Superintendent Rumage of the Red Bank found that bringing school-based administrators and several other members leadership team "provided them experience and perspective" on thinking about equity and analyzing data with an equity focus in their context. Rumage and his leadership team began "digging deeper into discipline data, attendance data, participation in athletic teams, and other types of data from a demographic lens."

From Scotch Plains-Fanwood, Joan Mast, assistant superintendent for curriculum, instruction, and technology, has frequently accompanied Superintendent Hayes to NJNS meetings. She shared that "this teamwork provided synergy for our district's equity initiatives," such as developing innovative approaches to basic skills instruction and encouraging a district-wide practice of disaggregating student data. One voice for equity in a school or district is more quickly amplified when other leaders share the commitment to act.

Practice Talking About Race

Becoming comfortable talking about inequities in general and racial inequities in particular is another critical area for leadership professional development. As we discussed in Chapter 4, leaders—and everyone else—need multiple, sustained opportunities in cross-racial groups to participate in dialogues on how race and racism are affecting students' educational experiences and outcomes. Open and explicit dialogue can help to identify and understand root causes of racism and inequity. These conversations also support educators in identifying practices and policies to address the causes that they have identified. Equity-focused leaders help their colleagues to recognize and disrupt conversations in which educators blame students of color, their families, or their communities. Instead, they expose beliefs, structures, practices, and policies that inequitably impact different student groups.

Practicing these types of dialogues in professional learning settings and in preservice preparation programs supports leaders to confront the kinds of situations they may encounter in their schools and districts. Role-play activities are one effective way to do so; for example, how to respond when a teacher makes a racist comment during a faculty meeting. This might involve an in-the-moment response, as well as following up privately with the teacher afterward. Trying out conversational "moves" in a learning community makes leaders more confident in calling out racist comments or instances of deficit thinking in their own practice, whether in a meeting or in one-on-one discussions with the educators with whom they work.

Leadership development initiatives, whether within a network, a university classroom, or a district's own professional development program, must deliberately create opportunities for regular discussions of race. With the skills and knowledge that leaders gain from conversations with their colleagues about race, they will be more likely to engage others productively when these types of situations occur; without them, they are likely to ignore or avoid addressing race and thus perpetuate systems that harm students of color.

The tenth end-of-the year meeting of NJNS illustrates the benefits of continued practice, even for committed, equity-focused leaders. A discussion about deficit thinking, using an activity from Edward Fergus's (2016) book, *Solving Disproportionality*, elicited a wide array of perspectives on the topic of immigration. The degree of difference in perspective surprised many participants and at times made some uncomfortable as their views were challenged. Assistant Superintendent Rachel Goldberg of Passaic Public Schools, who has attended several NJNS meetings in her current role and in her former role with Elizabeth Public Schools, reflected on how she could implement this type of activity in her district.

> *How do you address this range of opinions and ideas in a school system where you do not have the same level of comfort and trust? What happens when you have to confront the reality that your administrators or teachers have vastly different beliefs about race and equity without the safety net of a professional organization acting as a facilitator?*

Despite the challenges, district leaders have shared how they are using similar activities to encourage conversations about race and inequity in their districts. Goldberg added that "it is in the continuation of this work where we see leaders bravely address a multitude of opinions and come back to the network to share that it can be done. It is being done."

Open Up Classroom and School Doors

Professional learning is most effective when it is collaborative and embedded in day-to-day responsibilities of the job; this is true for both teachers and administrators (Peterson, 2002; Sparks & Hirsch, 2000). As teachers and administrators regularly open up their daily practices to colleagues, they strengthen their professional accountability to each other (Darling-Hammond, 1989) and support each other in moving from the culture of nice, discussed in Chapter 4, to a culture of direct and constructive feedback.

When schools or districts adopt practices such as equity visits, they support administrators and teachers in opening up their schools and classrooms to examine how issues of equity interact with instructional practices. Principal John Rivero of P.S. 5 in Jersey City Public Schools quickly volunteered to "be the guinea pig" when his district began to use instructional rounds and, later, equity visits. As he thinks back to inviting district staff into his building to host the first visit, he reflects,

> *A lot of district senior staff members descended on the school. Supervisors, the superintendent, they all were here. It was just an eye-opener, in terms of having people come to your building and give you feedback on what they see. Overall, it was a positive experience. I realized that you can't work in a vacuum. You have to have different stakeholders be a part of the process and give feedback.*

Historically, teaching has been a largely solitary practice in the United States, with each teacher at work in their own classroom, only rarely seeing how others teach. The same has been true for each principal in their own building. Practices such as equity visits have encouraged opening many classroom and schoolhouse doors, and to opening many principals' and superintendents' offices and meeting rooms. In the process, inequities that have always been there have become more visible, and educational leaders have begun the challenging work of addressing them.

ALL MEANS ALL

For too long, school and district policies and practices have reflected lower expectations for students of color and other underserved students. Educators and policymakers blame students and their families for low achievement, for not trying hard enough, or for not caring about school. Educational leaders have too often ignored inequities within their own systems, as well as within society, that have shaped students' experiences, opportunities, and outcomes. It is not possible to quantify the harm that this lack of attention has done to children, nor is it possible to quantify what this country has lost in terms of these children's potential.

The equity visits we describe in this book provide educational leaders with a resource for confronting and addressing educational inequities in their own schools and districts. But the tools have value only if educators choose to become equity warriors. While the moral imperative for equity belongs to all, principals and superintendents are uniquely positioned to lead. In our view, true equity-focused educational leaders are those who accept responsibility for imagining and creating schools and systems as they should be rather than blaming others, especially students and their families, for how they are now.

On their own, equity visits will not ameliorate the effects of broader structural forces that have isolated, oppressed, and marginalized groups of people because of their race, ethnicity, language, nationality, or income. However, they do represent a practical, field-tested way for leaders to examine how their schools inhibit some students' learning, work with other stakeholders in developing strategies that address inequities in their schools and classrooms, and contribute to creating systems that prepare all students. In these systems, students' demographics will not predict their outcomes. In these systems, ALL truly means ALL.

APPENDIX A
Participating Superintendents and Districts[1]

Dr. Brian Osborne, Currently, Lehigh University, College of Education; Prior, New Rochelle Public Schools (NY) and School District of South Orange and Maplewood

Brian Osborne served as superintendent of the South Orange Maplewood School District for seven years before taking on the superintendency in New Rochelle, NY. Prior to that, he served as chief of staff for teaching and learning in the New York City school system, and he has devoted more than 25 years to education as a teacher and administrator. He currently works as a professor of practice at Lehigh University's College of Education.

The School District of South Orange and Maplewood, NJ, serves about 6,900 students, about 44% of whom are African American and about 47% white, with the remaining 9% divided between Asian and Hispanic.

Dr. Carol L. Kelley, Currently, Oak Park Elementary School District 97 (IL); Prior, Branchburg Township School District

Carol L. Kelley, who is now superintendent of Oak Park Elementary School District 97 in Illinois, was superintendent of Branchburg Township School District, NJ, when she was a member of NJNS. Kelley had previously served as director of curriculum and instruction with Hunterdon Central Regional High School District in New Jersey and vice president of educational services for Edison Learning.

Branchburg Township School District serves about 2,300 students, 86% of whom are white, 4% Hispanic, 3% Black, and 7% Asian. Three percent qualify for free or reduced-price lunch.

Charles Sampson, Freehold Regional High School District

Charles Sampson has worked in a variety of administrative capacities including the positions of social studies supervisor, K–12, assistant principal for curricular initiatives, scheduling and facilities oversight, and high school principal. He served as superintendent of Verona Public School (NJ) prior to becoming superintendent of Freehold Regional High School District.

---

[1]Unless noted, all school districts are located in New Jersey.

Freehold Regional High School District, the largest regional high school district in New Jersey, serves approximately 10,500 students in six high schools across eight communities in Western Monmouth County, NJ. The diversity evident within the eight communities represents students from a wide range of backgrounds, with approximately 77% of students being white, 9% Asian/Pacific Islander, 10% Hispanic, and 5% Black. Close to 11% of students qualify for free or reduced-price meals.

Dr. Daniel Fishbein, Ridgewood Public Schools

Daniel Fishbein has been superintendent for the Ridgewood Public Schools since 2008. Prior to that he was superintendent for the Glen Ridge Public Schools for seven years. Prior to becoming a superintendent, Fishbein served as a high school principal, assistant principal, athletic director, science teacher, and coach.

Ridgewood serves about 5,800 students, with a demographic breakdown of 78% white, 17% Asian, 4% Hispanic, and 1% Black. Less than 3% of students qualify for free or reduced-price meals.

Dr. David Aderhold, West Windsor-Plainsboro Regional School District

David Aderhold became superintendent of West Windsor-Plainsboro Regional School District in 2013 after serving as deputy superintendent and assistant superintendent for pupil services and planning in the district. Prior to that, Aderhold has worked in a number of districts, including North Brunswick and New Brunswick, serving as a teacher, assistant principal, and high school principal.

West Windsor-Plainsboro Regional District serves about 10,000 students. About 67% are Asian, 21% white, 5% Black, and 5% Hispanic, and about 3% qualify for free or reduced-price lunch.

Earl Kim, Currently, Stamford Public Schools (CT); Prior, Montgomery Township Public Schools

Earl Kim has been the Superintendent for the Stamford Public Schools in Connecticut since 2016. Prior to that he was the head of school for the Kamehameha Schools – Kapālama in Hawaii and superintendent in the Montgomery Township Public Schools and Verona Schools in New Jersey. Kim has also served as a school trustee, principal, assistant principal, teacher, club advisor, coach, and U.S. Marine. He was an NJNS member while serving as superintendent in Montgomery Township Public Schools.

Montgomery Township Public Schools serves about 5,000 students, of whom approximately 70% are white, 25% Asian, 35% Hispanic, and 3% white, with 2% qualifying for free or reduced-price meals.

Dr. Jacqueline A. Young, Retired, Essex Regional Services Commission

Jacqueline Young served as superintendent of Essex Regional Educational Services Commission (ERESC) for 24 years before she retired. She began her career as an elementary school teacher in the Newark Public School District and the East Orange School District, before joining the New York Department of Education as a basic skills consultant and later, a school program coordinator. She joined ERESC in 1982 as a supervisor of instruction and became superintendent 10 years later.

The Essex Regional Educational Services Commission (ERESC) is a receiving school district. The majority of students who are sent to ERESC have underperformed on state assessments and are not functioning at grade level, and are many grade levels behind. Additionally, some have behavioral challenges and have experienced trauma. ERESC schools provide instructional services to over 300 students. More than 95% of the students are of African American or Latinx descent. Ninety-five percent of the students are male and from low socioeconomic backgrounds. All students participate in the free and reduced-price lunch program.

Dr. Jared Rumage, Red Bank Borough Public Schools

Jared Rumage has been the superintendent for the Red Bank Borough Public School District since 2014. Prior to becoming superintendent, he served the community of Woodbridge Township as a middle school principal, elementary school principal, director of high school athletics, teacher of special education, and varsity soccer coach.

The Red Bank Borough Public Schools serve about 1,400 students in preschool through Grade 8. The district demographics are 80% Hispanic, 10% white, 8% Black, and 2% other. Nearly 90% of the students qualify for free or reduced-price meals.

Dr. Jeffrey Moore, Hunterdon Central Regional High School District

Jeffrey Moore serves as the superintendent of Hunterdon Central Regional High School District. Moore comes to Hunterdon Central after serving 10 years as a central office administrator with the Freehold Regional High School District. During his 23 years in education, he has served as a director of curriculum and instruction, a strategic planning coordinator and consultant, a technology supervisor, an assessment coordinator, a high school social studies teacher, and more.

Hunterdon Central Regional High School District serves almost 3,000 students. About 10% are economically disadvantaged, and 2% are English language learners. Over 80% of students are white, 9% are Hispanic, 6% are Asian, and 3% are Black.

Dr. Joanne Mullane, Hopatcong Borough Schools

Joanne Mullane served as acting superintendent and director of curriculum and instruction for Hopatcong Borough Schools during her time with NJNS. Prior to that, Mullane served in many different capacities in the district, including professional development and the integration of new technologies in the district.

Hopatcong Borough Schools has a student population of 1,589 students, including 75% white, 17% Hispanic, 5% Black, and 3% Asian, with an economically disadvantaged population of 29% and a special education population of 22%.

John Kenyon Kummings, Wildwood Public Schools

Kenyon Kummings is currently the superintendent for Wildwood Public Schools and has been a member of NJNS since 2016. Prior to becoming superintendent, he was the principal of the elementary school in Wildwood for seven years. During his 15-year career in public education, he has always worked with urban populations and has fought to correct inequities that impact his students. Being an advocate for those with the greatest need is a personal goal that continues to drive his practice.

Wildwood Public Schools serves 880 students preK through 12th grade, with a population where 80% qualify for free and reduced-price lunch; 24% white; 62% Hispanic, 14% Black, and 0.2% Asian. In the most recent U.S. Census Bureau's Small Area Income and Poverty Estimates (SAIPE) report, Wildwood has been identified as having the highest ratio of students ages 5–17 living in poverty in the state of New Jersey.

Dr. John Ramos, Currently, Equity and Excellence Imperative; Prior, School District of South Orange and Maplewood

John Ramos retired as superintendent of the School District of South Orange and Maplewood in June of 2017. He had served in three previous superintendencies two principalships and worked with the Occupational Industrialization Center (O.I.C.), the Urban League, and two state departments of education. Throughout his career, he has held equity and excellence as nonnegotiable standards and has prioritized ethics and integrity as foundational to any good work. He currently works as a leadership consultant with the Equity and Excellence Imperative.

The School District of South Orange and Maplewood, NJ, serves about 6,900 students, about 44% of whom are African American and about 47% white, with the remaining 9% divided between Asian and Hispanic.

Dr. Jorden Schiff, Hillsborough Township Public Schools

Jorden Schiff has served as the Hillsborough Township Superintendent of Schools since 2011 and was the superintendent of

Readington Township for five years. He has experience as an assistant superintendent, principal, supervisor, vice principal, and teacher.

Hillsborough Township Public Schools is a high-performing suburban district located in central New Jersey with 7,400 students spanning preschool to 12th grade, and a demographic breakdown of 4% Black, 8% Hispanic, 30% Asian, and 58% white. Approximately 7% of students qualify for free or reduced-price meals.

Dr. Laurie W. Newell, Essex Regional Educational Services Commission

Laurie W. Newell is currently the superintendent of Essex Regional Educational Services Commission. She most recently served as the chief reform and innovations officer/assistant superintendent for the Paterson Public Schools, the third largest school district in New Jersey. She is a professional educator with experiences including as a National Science Foundation (NSF) teaching fellow, researcher, innovator, and district-level change agent. She has an enhanced understanding of the issues faced by large urban school districts, and these experiences have motivated her to find innovative ways to increase the capacity for learning and development via human capital resource management and talent development.

The Essex Regional Educational Services Commission (ERESC) is a receiving school district. The majority of students who are sent to ERESC have underperformed on state assessments and are not functioning at grade level, and are many grade levels behind. Additionally, some have behavioral challenges and have experienced trauma. ERESC schools provide instructional services to over 300 students. More than 95% of the students are of African American or Latinx descent. Ninety-five percent of the students are male and from low socio-economic backgrounds. All students participate in the free and reduced-price lunch program.

Dr. Marcia Lyles, Jersey City Public Schools

Marcia Lyles began her career as an English teacher in New York City Public Schools and then moved into administration, serving as assistant principal, principal, deputy superintendent, superintendent, regional superintendent, and deputy chancellor for teaching and learning. She then served as the superintendent for the Christina School District in Delaware before taking on the superintendency in Jersey City.

Jersey City Public Schools is a racially, ethnically, and socioeconomically diverse preK through 12th grade district of almost 30,000 students. The population is 38% Latinx, 32% Black, 16% Asian, and 10% white, and 68% of students are economically disadvantaged.

Dr. Margaret W. Hayes, Scotch Plains-Fanwood Public Schools

Margaret W. Hayes is the superintendent of schools for Scotch Plains-Fanwood Public Schools. With experience that spans both public and private education, she has previously served as a secondary social studies and English teacher, dean, K–12 supervisor, elementary school principal, assistant superintendent, and adjunct instructor at the collegiate level. Building on over 35 years of experience in education, she continues to seek ways to improve learning and teaching, recognizing that our future rests on how well we prepare the students of today for a world that has yet to be imagined.

Scotch Plains-Fanwood Public Schools serves over 5,000 students. Sixty-six percent of the students are white, about 13% are Hispanic, 10% Asian, 7% Black, and 4% are two or more races. Five percent of the students are economically disadvantaged.

Dr. Michael R. Gorman, Currently, Salem Community College; Retired, Pemberton Township Schools

Michael Gorman, who is now serving as the president of Salem Community College, was superintendent of Pemberton Township Schools during his time as member of the NJNS. Prior to 2007, when his superintendency in Pemberton began, Mike was superintendent of Glassboro Public Schools, NJ. He has also served as deputy superintendent, principal, teacher, and coach.

Pemberton Township Schools serves about 5,000 students, of whom close to 44% qualify for free or reduced-price lunch. The racial/ethnic breakdown is as follows: 13% Hispanic, 30% Black, 55% White, and 2% Asian.

Nancy Gartenberg, Montgomery Township School District

Nancy Gartenberg is the superintendent of Montgomery Township School District. Prior to that, she served as superintendent of South Hunterdon High School for five years. She came to Hunterdon from Hamilton Township School District in Mercer County, where she taught math, science, and reading in Grice Middle School and was head boys' varsity swim coach and jayvee girls' soccer coach at Hamilton High School West.

Montgomery Township Public Schools serves about 5,000 students, of whom approximately 70% are white, 25% Asian, 35 Hispanic, and 3% Black, with 2% qualifying for free or reduced-price meals.

Olga Hugelmeyer, Elizabeth Public Schools

Olga Hugelmeyer has been the superintendent for the Elizabeth Public Schools since 2013. Prior to that she was the assistant superintendent for the district for six years. Hugelmeyer also served as a director of early childhood education, supervisor of grants, math facilitator, and elementary bilingual teacher.

The Elizabeth Public Schools serves about 28,717 students, with a demographic breakdown of 71% Hispanic, 19% Black, 8% white, 2% Asian, with 0.8% other. Over 81% of students qualify for free meals and reduced-price meals.

Pablo Muñoz, Currently, Passaic Public Schools; Prior, Elizabeth Public Schools

Pablo Muñoz has served as the superintendent of schools for the Passaic Public Schools since 2013. He served as superintendent of schools in the Elizabeth Public Schools from 2005 to 2013. In both roles, he was a member of NJNS.

Passaic Public Schools has a diverse student body, with the ethnicity of students being Hispanic 93%, Black 4%, Asian 2%, Pacific Islander 0.15%, white 1%, and American Indian 0.06%. Of this total student population, 14% represent special education students, and 25% represent Limited-English Proficient (LEP) students. Eighty-nine percent of students are eligible for free and reduced-priced meals.

Dr. Patrick Amiot P. Michel, Salem City School District

Patrick Michel received his doctorate in educational leadership from Seton Hall University. He has served as superintendent of Salem City School District since 2009. Some hallmarks of his tenure include increasing graduation rates by over 15% and having Salem High School become an IB World School through the offering of the International Baccalaureate Diploma Programme since 2012.

Salem City School District's three schools serve 1,132 students, with a demographic breakdown of 72% Black, 13% White, 12% Hispanic, and <1% Asian/American Indian or Alaskan Native. About 85% of students qualify for free or reduced-price meals.

Dr. Rocco Tomazic, Freehold Borough School District

Rocco Tomazic is a retired U.S. Navy commander who brought his leadership experience to his educational career. He spent 17 years in the Linden Public Schools, including four as superintendent. Tomazic currently serves as superintendent of Freehold Borough School District, bringing two decades of instructional and administrative experience to his role.

Freehold Borough is a preK–8 district that feeds into the Freehold Regional High School District. The district serves 1,700 students, with a demographic breakdown of 77% Hispanic, 12% white, 9% Black, and 2% Asian.

Dr. Samuel Stewart, Retired, Mercer County

Samuel Stewart retired as executive county superintendent of Mercer County after over 40 years of managerial and leadership experience in both the private and public education sectors. This included serving as a junior high school teacher and principal, headmaster of an independent school, assistant superintendent, and superintendent in Ridgewood Village School District, South Brunswick School District, Randolph, Township Schools, and Montgomery Township Public Schools.

Mercer County includes 13 municipalities, including Princeton and Trenton, representing a diverse range of student populations, district structures, and town property wealth. The county superintendent supervises and administers the county office of education as a representative of the state commissioner of education.

Dr. Tami Crader, Neptune School District

Tami Crader has been the superintendent in Neptune Township Schools in Monmouth County since 2015. Prior to her current position, she served as superintendent in Warren Township, assistant superintendent in Readington Township, and principal and vice principal in Marlboro Township.

Neptune Township is a district that serves over 4,000 students, about half of whom receive free and reduced meals with a demographic breakdown of 61% Black, 12% Hispanic, 24% white, and 3% other.

Dr. Victoria Spirko Kniewel, Currently, Edgemont School District (NY); Prior, West Windsor-Plainsboro Regional District

Victoria Kniewel is currently superintendent of schools in the Edgemont School District, Scarsdale, NY. She was superintendent of West Windsor-Plainsboro Regional District, NJ, during her years of membership with NJNS. She began her career as a teacher, and after teaching for 17 years, Kniewel served as principal in the Ridgewood Public School District, assistant superintendent and principal for the Ho-Ho-Kus Public School District, and assistant superintendent for curriculum and personnel for the North Salem Central School District North Salem, NY.

West Windsor-Plainsboro Regional District serves about 10,000 students. About 67% are Asian, 21% white, 5% Black, and 5% Hispanic, and about 3% qualify for free or reduced-price lunch.

APPENDIX B
Resources

INITIATING CONVERSATIONS ON RACE

- *Black Participatory Research: Power, Identity, and the Struggle for Justice in Education* (2016). Elizabeth R. Drame and Decoteau J. Irby (Eds.). New York, NY: Palgrave Macmillan.

- *Cultural Proficiency: A Manual for School Leaders* (2018). Randall B. Lindsey, Kikanza Nuri-Robins, Raymond D. Terrell, and Delores B. Lindsey. Thousand Oaks, CA: Corwin.

- *Courageous Conversations About Race: A Field Guide for Achieving Equity in Schools* (2006). Glenn E. Singleton and Curtis W. Linton. Thousand Oaks, CA: Corwin.

- *Courageous Conversations About Race: A Field Guide for Achieving Equity in Schools* (2nd ed.) (2014). Glenn E. Singleton. Thousand Oaks, CA: Corwin.

- *Solving Disproportionality and Achieving Equity: A Leader's Guide to Using Data to Change Hearts and Minds* (2016). Edward Fergus. Thousand Oaks, CA: Corwin.

CONDUCTING INSTRUCTIONAL ROUNDS

- *Instructional Rounds in Education: A Network Approach to Improving Teaching and Learning* (2009). Elizabeth A. City, Richard F. Elmore, Sarah E. Fiarman, and Lee Teitel. Cambridge, MA: Harvard Education Press.

- *Leading Instructional Rounds in Education: A Facilitator's Guide* (2013). Thomas Fowler-Finn. Cambridge, MA: Harvard Education Press.

- *Instructional Rounds in Action* (2012). John E. Roberts. Cambridge, MA: Harvard Education Press.

- *School-Based Instructional Rounds: Improving Teaching and Learning Across Classrooms* (2013). Lee Teitel. Cambridge, MA: Harvard Education Press.

USING PROTOCOLS

- *The Facilitator's Book of Questions: Tools for Looking Together at Teacher and Student Work* (2004). David Allen and Tina Blythe. New York: Teachers College Press.

- *Facilitating for Learning: Tools for Teacher Groups of All Kinds* (2016). David Allen and Tina Blythe. New York: Teachers College Press.

- *Looking Together at Student Work* (3rd ed) (2015). Tina Blythe, David Allen, and Barbara Schieffelin Powell. New York: Teachers College Press.

- *The Power of Protocols: An Educator's Guide to Better Practice* (3rd ed.) (2013). Joseph P. McDonald, Nancy Mohr, Alan Dichter, and Elizabeth C. McDonald. New York: Teachers College Press.

- The School Reform Initiative, available at https://www .schoolreforminitiative.org/

EQUITY-FOCUSED DATA ANALYSIS

- Equity Audits (2018). The Mid-Atlantic Equity Consortium, available at https://maec.org/resource/equity-audit-materials/

- *Solving Disproportionality and Achieving Equity: A Leader's Guide to Using Data to Change Hearts and Minds* (2016). Edward Fergus. Thousand Oaks, CA: Corwin.

- "Community-Based Equity Audits: A Practical Approach for Educational Leaders to Support Equitable Community-School Improvements" (2017). Terrance L. Green. *Educational Administration Quarterly*, 53(1), 3–39.

- Racial Equity Tools, available at http://www.racialequitytools.org/ plan/issues/education

- *Using Equity Audits to Create Equitable and Excellent Schools* (2009). Linda E. Skrla, Kathryn B. McKenzie, and James Joseph Scheurich (Eds.). Thousand Oaks, CA: Corwin.

- *Building Equity: Policies and Practices to Empower All Learners* (2017). Dominique Smith, Nancy Frey, and Ian Pumpian. Alexandria, VA: Association for Supervision and Curriculum Development.

LEADING FOR EQUITY STORIES FROM THE FIELD

- *Detracking for Excellence and Equity* (2008). Carol Corbett Burris and Delia T. Garrity. Alexandria, VA: Association for Supervision and Curriculum Development.

- *Leading for Equity: The Pursuit of Excellence in the Montgomery County Public Schools* (2009). Stacey M. Childress, Denis P. Doyle, and David A. Thomas. Cambridge, MA: Harvard Education Press.

- *Culturally Responsive School Leadership* (2018). Muhammad Khalifa. Cambridge, MA: Harvard Education Press.

- *Every Child, Every Classroom, Every Day: School Leaders Who Are Making Equity a Reality* (2011). Robert Peterkin, Deborah Jewell-Sherman, Laura Kelley, and Leslie Boozer. San Francisco, CA: John Wiley & Sons.

- *Latino Educational Leadership: Serving Latino Communities and Preparing Latinx Leaders Across the P-20 Pipeline* (2018). Cristóbal Rodríguez, Melissa A Martinez, and Fernando Valle (Eds). Charlotte, NC: Information Age Publishing.

- *The School Leaders Our Children Deserve: Seven Keys to Equity, Social Justice, and School Reform* (2009). George Theoharis. New York: Teachers College Press.

- *Advancing Equity and Achievement in America's Diverse Schools: Inclusive Theories, Policies, and Practices* (2014). Camille M. Wilson and Sonya Douglass Horsford. New York: Routledge.

MORE ON THE NEW JERSEY NETWORK OF SUPERINTENDENTS

- "Creating Equitable Outcomes in a Segregated State" (2019). Thomas Hatch, Rachel Roegman, and David Allen. *Phi Delta Kappan*. Available at https://www.kappanonline.org/creating-equitable-outcomes-segregated-state-hatch-roegman-allen/

- "Equity Goals and Equity Visits: Leaders in a Superintendent Network Jointly Study Each Other's Diverse Schools to Pursue High-Leverage Academic Goals" (2017). Thomas Hatch and Rachel Roegman. *School Administrator, 10*(74), 39–41. Available at https://my.aasa.org/AASA/Resources/SAMag/2017/Nov17/HatchRoegman.aspx

- "Out of Isolation: Superintendents Band Together to Improve Instruction and Equity in Their Districts" (2012). Thomas Hatch and Rachel Roegman. *Journal of Staff Development, 33*(6), 37–41. Available at https://www.learningforward.org/docs/jsd-december-2012/hatch336.pdf

- "NJNS and Elizabeth Public Schools" (2011). Rachel D. Kliegman (Roegman). *Strategies for School System Leaders on District-Level Change, 15*(1), 15–19. Available at http://www.aasa.org/uploadedFiles/Resources/Other_Resources/StrategiesNov-2011.pdf

- "A Network Approach to Developing System-Level Instructional Leadership" (2011). Larry Leverett and Scott Thompson. *Strategies for School System Leaders on District-Level Change, 15*(1), 1–2. Available at http://www.aasa.org/uploadedFiles/Resources/Other_Resources/StrategiesNov-2011.pdf

- "The AP Lever for Boosting Access, Success, and Equity" (2016). Rachel Roegman and Thomas Hatch. *Phi Delta Kappan, 97*(5), 20–25. Available at https://journals.sagepub.com/doi/10.1177/0031721716629653

- "Reversing Course: Equity-Focused Leadership in Action" (2019). Charles Sampson, Jeffery Moore, and Rachel Roegman. *Educational Leadership, 76*(6), 58–63. Available at http://www.ascd.org/publications/educational_leadership/mar19/vol76/num06/Reversing_Course@_Equity-Focused_Leadership_in_Action.aspx

- "Core Practices Fuel Superintendents' Equity Focus" (2016). Scott Thompson. *The Learning Professional, 37*(6), 32–36.

- "A Community of System-Level Instructional Leaders" (2011). Scott Thompson. *Strategies for School System Leaders on District-Level Change, 15*(1), 3–14. Available at http://www.aasa.org/uploadedFiles/Resources/Other_Resources/StrategiesNov-2011.pdf

- "Becoming Agents of Change for Incarcerated Youth: Superintendents Working to Disrupt the School-to-Prison Pipeline" (2018). Jacqueline Young, Larry Leverett, and Rachel Roegman. *Ragazine*. Available at http://ragazine.cc/2018/05/agents-of-change-disrupting-school-to-prison-pipeline/

 Available for download at resources.corwin.com/equityvisits

APPENDIX C
Tools and Resources

EQUITY VISIT SCHEDULE TEMPLATE

Time	Minutes*	Activity
	20	Breakfast and Welcome
	40	Overview of Equity Focus and Problem of Practice
	25	Divide Into Observing Teams and Assign Roles
	90	Classroom Visits
	30	Interviews of Students and/or Teachers
	60	Small Group Debriefs (see Patterns and Wonderings Protocol)
	45	Lunch
	60	Small Group Report Out Patterns and Wonderings to Whole Group
	45	Host Fishbowl (see Appendix D: Fishbowl Protocol)
	20	Observer Reflections on the Day (see Appendix D: Learning Journal Template)

*Note: Host puts in actual times based on school start time. Times should be modified based on passing schedules, need for transportation to different sites, and other local particulars.

online resources ⏷ Available for download at resources.corwin.com/equityvisits

ASSIGNING ROLES FOR SMALL GROUPS TEMPLATE

	Group A	Group B	Group C	Group D	Group E
Facilitator/Time Keeper					
Teacher Observer					
Student Observer					
Content Observer					

online resources

Available for download at resources.corwin.com/equityvisits

Roles and Responsibilities

Facilitator/Timekeeper – Keeps group on task and on time. Ensures each member of the group has opportunity to contribute to discussions. Observes whole-class dynamics/ structure and any other aspects related to equity or the instructional core.

Teacher Observer(s) – Focuses attention on the teacher(s); notes their actions, comments, and questions; focuses on teacher-specific look-fors.

Student Observer(s) – Focuses attention on observing the students and their interactions with the teacher and with other students; notes student engagement with tasks; focuses on student-specific look-fors; talks to three to five students during the observation (assuming students are doing independent or group work—does not talk to students during whole-class discussion, lecture, or test).

Content Observer(s) – Focuses attention on the nature of the tasks given to students, posted or stated standards or objectives; posted student work or artifacts, such as portfolios, worksheets, etc.; focuses on content/task-specific look-fors.

TAKING NOTES DURING CLASSROOM OBSERVATIONS TEMPLATE

Equity Focus:

Problem of Practice:

Classroom Context Information (grade, subject, etc.):

Look-Fors	Evidence Collected
What evidence is there that the <u>**teacher**</u>: • • •	
What evidence is there that the <u>**students**</u>: • • •	
What evidence is there that the <u>**content or task**</u>: • • •	

*Note: The equity focus, problem of practice, and look-fors should be filled in by the host leadership team prior to the visit.

 Available for download at resources.corwin.com/equityvisits

LEARNING JOURNAL TEMPLATE

What "aha" moments or insights did you have?

What remains unclear or what new questions do you have?

How can we increase our individual and collective learning in future meetings?

online resources

Available for download at resources.corwin.com/equityvisits

EQUITY FOCUS FEEDBACK TEMPLATE

Note: In NJNS, facilitators provide participants with a PowerPoint document with these slides. All superintendents along with leadership team members, fill in the slides with their own district work. The slides (often distributed in hard-copy packets as well) are used to focus and support their presentation in the Learning Together Consultancy Protocol (see Appendix D).

Slide 1:

Context

- Demographics and other important context information about my district/schools/community

---

Slide 2:

What is my district's current equity focus?

- How does it align with district and school goals and strategic planning for instructional improvement?

- How are we communicating it with key district stakeholders (leadership team, Board, community, etc.)?

Slide 3:

What key data are we using to define and address our equity focus?

- How are we disaggregating the data?

Slide 4:

What progress have we made in addressing our equity focus this school year?

Slide 5:

**What is one obstacle/challenge/question
we would like feedback on in addressing our equity focus?**

 Available for download at resources.corwin.com/equityvisits

DEVELOPING PATTERNS AND WONDERINGS PROTOCOL

This protocol is used by small teams during equity visits, after the teams have observed in classrooms, conducted interviews, and completed other evidence collection activities. It typically takes 50–60 minutes.

PURPOSES

To support teams of participants in an equity visit (or related practice) in:

- Reviewing evidence collected from various data collection activities.
- Developing patterns and wonderings to share with the host leadership team.

ROLES

- Each small group (4–5 participants) includes:
    - *Facilitator*—Supports the group's process, including reviewing purposes, introducing and transitioning between steps, and keeping time.
    - *Recorder*—Records the patterns and wonderings (usually as a set of bullet points on chart paper or in an electronic document).
    - *Presenter*—Reports briefly on the group's patterns and wonderings in the whole-group share out; answers any clarifying questions from the whole group.

Note: Facilitator, recorder, and presenter also participate in discussion.

MATERIALS

- Copies of the protocol

- Chart paper and markers for each small group (or a laptop/tablet)
- Individuals' note-taking sheets from data collection activities

STEPS

- *Review purpose, roles, and steps (by facilitator)—2–3 min.*
- *Review of evidence collected—5 min.*
  - Each team member reviews their notes, identifying possible patterns and wonderings related to the problem of practice and equity focus.
- *Develop patterns & wonderings—40–45 min.*
  - Individuals take turns sharing evidence related to the problem of practice. This may be done in a number of ways, including
    - By evidence collection role, i.e., evidence related to students, evidence related to teachers, evidence related to content
    - Classroom-by-classroom, i.e., team members share evidence in relation to each classroom visited, typically in the order they were visited
  - Teams consider how evidence from interviews and other evidence collection activities relate to patterns/wonderings and/or suggest additional patterns/wonderings.
  - Recorder charts emerging patterns and wonderings.

Notes:

- Teams often spend the bulk of time on identifying patterns, saving at least 5 or 10 minutes for wonderings.
- Patterns are typically grouped by instructional core category: *Student, Teacher, Content.*
- All patterns shared in the large group should be supported by evidence the team agrees on.
- No individual teachers, students, or other individuals should be identified in the patterns or wonderings.

- *Debrief process—3–5 min.*
  - Facilitator leads brief reflection on how process of protocol worked for group, including suggestions for using it in the future.

online resources — Available for download at resources.corwin.com/equityvisits

FISHBOWL PROTOCOL

This protocol is used during equity visits to support the host team in beginning to consider the patterns and wonderings that are shared by the small groups. It allows the full group to "listen in on" this discussion. The discussion is not intended to resolve the issues that have arisen in the patterns and wonderings or develop an action plan, but rather initiate discussions and planning that will continue within the school/district.

Space should be organized so that fishbowl participants are sitting in a circle/oval and can easily see and hear one another; reflectors sit outside the circle but should be able to hear the fishbowl participants' discussion. Completed chart paper with patterns and wonderings from teams should be visible to fishbowl participants. Typically, this takes 35–45 minutes.

PURPOSES

To support host team in:

- Reflecting on patterns and wonderings shared by observation teams.

- Thinking through initial ideas, hypotheses, and questions related to the equity focus and problem of practice to be explored in more depth in subsequent meetings and activities.

ROLES

- *Facilitator*—Supports the group's process, including reviewing purposes, reminding group of roles, and keeping time. Does not participate in discussion itself, but may intervene to refocus group on purposes for fishbowl.

- *Fishbowl Leader*—*typically the host superintendent or principal.* Briefly initiates the discussion within the fishbowl and ensures that all participants within the fishbowl share their perspectives.

- *Fishbowl Participants*—Members of the host leadership team.

- *Recorder*—One fishbowl participant takes notes for future reference (typically, not on chart paper).

- *Reflectors*—Participants on visiting teams.

MATERIALS

- Copies of the protocol

STEPS

- *Review purpose, roles, and steps (by facilitator)*—2–3 min.
- *Initiation of fishbowl discussion*—1 min.
  - Fishbowl leader asks fishbowl participants to reflect on patterns and observations that are most urgent or compelling for them—and why.
- *Fishbowl discussion*—25–30 min.
  - Fishbowl participants take turns reflecting on patterns and wonderings. This may be done in a go-round (i.e., in order) or "popcorn" style (i.e., as participants choose to speak).
  - Fishbowl leader (or anyone inside the fishbowl group) may ask clarifying questions.
  - In the final 5–10 minutes of the protocol, fishbowl leader may synthesize some of the questions or issues for further discussion.
  - Recorder keeps track of emerging questions, issues, and ideas.

  Notes:

  - Reflectors do not interrupt or interact with participants during discussion.

  - Facilitator may remind fishbowl leader and participants of the purpose if the fishbowl discussion appears to becoming largely explanatory (i.e., for reflectors' benefit) or defensive.

- *Debrief process*—3–5 min.
  - Facilitator leads brief reflection on how process of protocol worked for group, including suggestions for using it in the future.

 Available for download at resources.corwin.com/equityvisits

NEXT STEPS PROTOCOL

This protocol is typically used at the end of an equity visit. It is intended as a brainstorm to generate many possible ideas for the host team to consider in subsequent meetings, not as a structure for creating a concrete plan.

It can be conducted as a full-group discussion, but for groups larger than 8, it is more effective to break into smaller groups of 4 or 5 participants. It takes approximately 50–60 minutes to complete.

PURPOSE

- To support host teams in developing short-, medium-, and longer-term goals and strategies based on feedback from an equity visit.

ROLES

- Each small group (4–5 participants) includes:
  - *Facilitator*—Supports the group's process, including reviewing purposes, introducing and transitioning between steps, and keeping time.
  - *Equity visit observers*—Responsible for drawing on their professional experience to offer recommendations.
  - *Recorder*—Records the group's agreed-upon possible next steps; presents to the larger group.

Note: Host leadership team members are encouraged to listen actively and reflect on potential next steps identified.

MATERIALS

- Copies of the protocol
- Chart paper and markers for each small group

STEPS

- *Review purpose, roles, and steps (by facilitator)—2–3 min.*
- *Individual brainstorming—5–7 min.*
  - Observers individually brainstorm possible action items for short-, medium-, and long-term goals and strategies.

- *Developing suggestions—20–25 min.*
  - o In small groups, observers develop a small set of suggestions for each designated time period: short, medium, longer term (e.g. 30, 90, and 180 days). Groups may use different strategies, including:
    - ▪ Individuals take turns sharing their short-, medium-, and longer-term suggestions, while others listen.
    - ▪ Groups focus on each period, discussing suggestions from all members for each period before moving on to the next.
  - o Recorder records final suggestions for each period on chart paper to share with host team and larger group.

Note: During this segment, host leadership team members may circulate, listening in on groups as they deliberate but not answering questions or otherwise interacting with groups.

- *Sharing suggestions—5–7 min.*
  - o The reporter from each group briefly shares suggestions for short-, medium-, and longer-term goals and strategies; answers clarifying questions.
- *Host leadership team reflections—5–10 min.*
  - o Members of the host leadership team briefly reflect on what they heard in suggestions.

Note: Members should not try to address every suggestion that came up or explain why a suggestion would not work, but rather focus on those that are most useful in supporting their thinking going forward.

- *Debrief process—3–5 min.*
  - o Facilitator leads brief reflection on how process of protocol worked for group, including suggestions for using it in the future.

 Available for download at resources.corwin.com/equityvisits

LEARNING TOGETHER CONSULTANCY PROTOCOL

Adapted from the Consultancy Protocol (developed by the School Reform Initiative; see Appendix B), this protocol is typically used to provide a host leadership team feedback in developing an equity goal, problem of practice, or strategy for achieving equity. It may be used to prepare for an equity visit or to reflect on strategies developed as result of an equity visit. It is usually conducted as a full group, with small groups developing feedback for the presenting team. It typically takes 75–90 minutes.

PURPOSE

- To focus deep analysis and reflection on a significant piece of a district's in-progress efforts focused on a problem of practice or equity focus related to equity and instruction.

Note: Not meant to be a showcasing of completed or exemplary work.

ROLES

- *Facilitator*—Supports process, including reviewing purposes, introducing and transitioning between steps, and keeping time.
- *Presenting team*—Members of school or district leadership team who have been involved in identifying the work-in-progress for feedback.
- *Reflectors*—All other participants.

Note: For larger groups, it is helpful to break into groups of 4 or 5 to develop feedback.

MATERIALS

- Copies of the protocol
- Chart paper and markers for each small group of reflectors
- Optional: Equity-Focused Feedback Template (see Appendix C)

STEPS

- *Review of purpose, roles, and steps (by facilitator)*—**3–5 mins.**

- *Presentation*—**15–20 mins.**
  - Possible topics for presenting team include:
    - Before an equity visit: data used to inform development of an equity focus or problem of practice: (e.g. student demographics, current strategies, professional development for teachers)
    - After an equity visit: initial plans or next steps in response to feedback from visit.

- *Questions for presenting team*—**10–20 mins.**
  - Reflectors ask clarifying questions; presenting team members respond briefly and factually (5–10 mins.).
    - *Clarifying questions* can generally be answered succinctly, sometimes with a yes or no answer. Example of a clarifying question: How many levels of Algebra 1 does the school now have?
  - Reflectors ask probing questions; presenting team members respond (5–10 mins.).
    - *Probing questions* require team members to think deeply, often questioning their assumptions. Example of a probing question: What factors do you believe are contributing to the underrepresentation of African American boys in Advanced Placement classes?

- *Feedback*—**20–25 mins.**
  - In small groups, reflectors discuss presentation and responses to questions and develop feedback for presenting team. Feedback includes "warm" comments, e.g., strengths or potential strengths in work-in-progress presented, as well as "cool" comments and questions, e.g., pointing to potential gaps, questioning assumptions, and suggesting changes related to presenting team's goal(s) (15–20 mins.).
    - A volunteer for each small group records feedback on chart paper.
  - Recorder for each group shares feedback comments in large group (5 mins.).

Variation: Members of the reflecting team circulate and listen in on small-group discussions but do not interact with groups as they develop feedback.

- ***Reflection*—10–15 mins.**
  - ○ Presenting team members reflect on the feedback, typically addressing a small number of comments or questions that are most relevant to their goal(s).

Variation: This segment can be conducted as a mini fishbowl discussion, with reflectors listening in on a discussion among the presenting team members.

- ***Debrief process*—5 mins.**
  - ○ Presenters and reflectors reflect on the process of using the protocol, including what changes/adjustments might make it more effective in future uses.

 Available for download at resources.corwin.com/equityvisits

REFERENCES

Allen, D., Roegman, R., & Hatch. T. (2015). Investigating discourses for administrators' learning within instructional rounds. *Educational Management Administration & Leadership*, *44*(5), 837–852.

Arao, B., & Clemens, K. (2013). From safe spaces to brave spaces: A new way to frame dialogue around diversity and social justice. In L. Landreman (Ed.), *The art of effective facilitation* (pp. 135–150). Sterling, VA: Stylus.

Argyris, C. (1977). Double loop learning in organizations. *Harvard Business Review*, *55*(5), 115–125.

Argyris, C., & Schön, D. (1974). *Theory in practice: Increasing professional effectiveness*. San Francisco, CA: Jossey-Bass.

Baldwin, J. (1962/2011). *The cross of redemption: Uncollected writings*. New York: Vintage Books.

Blackmore, J. (2009). Leadership for social justice: A transnational dialogue. *Journal of Research on Leadership Education*, *4*(1), 1–10.

Blythe, T., Allen, D., & Powell, B. S. (2015). *Looking together at student work* (3rd ed.). New York: Teachers College Press.

Bonilla-Silva, E. (2017). *Racism without racists: Color-blind racism and the persistence of racial inequality in America* (5th ed.). Lanham, MD: Rowman and Littlefield.

Brooks, J. S. (2007). Race and educational leadership: Conversation catalysts to prompt reflection, discussion, and action for individuals and organizations. *UCEA Review*, *67*(2), 1–3.

Bryk, A. S., & Schneider, B. (2003). Trust in schools: A core resource for school reform. *Educational Leadership*, *60*(6), 40–45.

Bush, G. W. (2000, July 10). *Speech to the NAACP*. Retrieved from http://www.washingtonpost.com/wp-srv/onpolitics/elections/bushtext071000.htm?noredirect=on

Carpenter, B. W., & Diem, S. (2013). Talking race: Facilitating critical conversations in educational leadership preparation programs. *Journal of School Leadership*, *23*(6), 902–931.

Carter, P. L., & Welner, K. G. (Eds.). (2013). *Closing the opportunity gap: What America must do to give every child an even chance*. Oxford, England: Oxford University Press.

Childress, S. M., Doyle, D. P., & Thomas, D. A. (2009). *Leading for equity: The pursuit of excellence in the Montgomery County Public Schools*. Cambridge, MA: Harvard Education Press.

City, E. A., Elmore, R. F., Fiarman, S. E., & Teitel, L. (2009). *Instructional rounds in education: A network approach to improving teaching and learning*. Cambridge, MA: Harvard Education Press.

Cohen, D. K., & Ball, D. L. (1999). *Instruction, capacity, and improvement*. CPRE Research Report Series RR-43. Philadelphia, PA: Consortium for Policy Research in Education, University of Pennsylvania.

Cohen-Vogel, L., & Osborne-Lampkin, L. T. (2007). Allocating quality: Collective bargaining agreements and administrative discretion over teacher assignment. *Educational Administration Quarterly*, *43*(4), 433–461.

Daresh, J. C., & Alexander, L. (2015). *Beginning the principalship: A practical guide for new school leaders*. Thousand Oaks, CA: Corwin.

Darling-Hammond, L. (1989). Accountability for professional practice. *Teachers College Record*, *91*(1), 59–80.

DiAngelo, R. (2011). White fragility. *International Journal of Critical Pedagogy*, *3*(3), 54–70.

DiAngelo, R. (2018). *White fragility: Why it's so hard for white people to talk about racism.* Boston, MA: Beacon Press.

Downey, C. J., Steffy, B. E., English, F. W., Frase, L. E., & Poston Jr., W. K. (Eds.). (2004). *The three-minute classroom walk-through: Changing school supervisory practice one teacher at a time.* Thousand Oaks, CA: Corwin.

Edmonds, R. (1979). Effective schools for the urban poor. *Educational Leadership*, *37*(1), 15–24.

Elmore, R. (2007). Professional networks and school improvement. *School Administrator*, *64*(4), 20–24.

Elmore, R. (2008). Practicing professionals/ Interviewer: Tracy Crow. *Journal of Staff Development*, *29*(2), 42–47.

Fair Housing & Equity Assessment Report. (2015). Retrieved from http://togethernor thjersey.com/wp-content/uploads/2015/08/FHEA_Report_031715.pdf

Fergus, E. (2016). *Solving disproportionality and achieving equity: A leader's guide to using data to change hearts and minds.* Thousand Oaks, CA: Corwin.

Ford, D. (2011). *Reversing underachievement among gifted Black students: Promising practices and programs.* New York: Teachers College Press.

Fowler-Finn, T. (2013). *Leading instructional rounds in education: A facilitator's guide.* Cambridge, MA: Harvard Education Press.

García, S. B., & Guerra, P. L. (2004). Deconstructing deficit thinking: Working with educators to create more equitable learning environments. *Education and Urban Society*, *36*(2), 150–168.

Gooden, M. A., & Dantley, M. (2012). Centering race in a framework for leadership preparation. *Journal of Research on Leadership Education*, *7*(2), 237–253.

Grissom, J. A., & Redding, C. (2015). Discretion and disproportionality: Explaining the underrepresentation of high-achieving students of color in gifted programs. *AERA Open*, *2*(1), 1–25.

Grossman, P., Wineburg, S., & Woolworth, S. (2001, December). Toward a theory of teacher community. *Teachers College Review*, *103*(6), 942–1012.

Hallinger, P. (2003). Leading educational change: Reflections on the practice of instructional and transformational leadership. *Cambridge Journal of Education*, *33*(3), 329–352.

Hatch, T., Hill, K., & Roegman, R. (2016). Investigating the role of instructional rounds in the development of social networks and district-wide improvement. *American Educational Research Journal*, *53*(4), 1022–1053.

Hawley, W., & James, R. (2010). Diversity-responsive school leadership. *UCEA Review*, *52*(3), 1–5.

Hobson, M. (2014). Color blind or color brave? TED2014 Talk. Retrieved from https://www.ted.com/talks/mellody_hobson_color_blind_or_color_brave/transcript?language=en

hooks, b. (1992). *Black looks: Race and representation.* Cambridge, MA: South End.

Ishimaru, A. (2013). From heroes to organizers: Principals and education organizing in urban school reform. *Educational Administration Quarterly*, *49*(1), 3–51.

Jean-Marie, G., Normore, A., & Brooks, J. S. (2009). Leadership for social justice: Preparing 21st century school leaders for a new social order. *Journal of Research on Leadership in Education*, *4*(1), 1–31.

Jones, C. (2002). Teachers' perceptions of African American principals' leadership in urban schools. *Peabody Journal of Education*, *77*(1), 7–34.

Karp, D. R., & Breslin, B. (2001). Restorative justice in school communities. *Youth & Society*, *33*(2), 249–272.

Khalifa, M. A., Jennings, M. E., Briscoe, F., Oleszweski, A. M., & Abdi, N. (2014). Racism? Administrative and community perspectives in data-driven decision making: Systemic perspectives versus technical-rational perspectives. *Urban Education, 49*(2), 147–182.

Ladson-Billings, G. (2006). From the achievement gap to the education debt: Understanding achievement in US schools. *Educational Researcher, 35*(7), 3–12.

Laughlin, P. R., Hatch, E. C., Silver, J. S., & Boh, L. (2006). Groups perform better than the best individuals on letters-to-numbers problems: Effects of group size. *Journal of Personality and Social Psychology, 90*(4), 644.

Leithwood, K., & Jantzi, D. (2000). The effects of transformational leadership on organizational conditions and student engagement with school. *Journal of Educational Administration, 38*(2), 112–129.

Leverett, L. (2002). Warriors to advance equity: An argument for distributing leadership. *Spotlight on student success* (Vol. 709). Calverton, MD: Mid-Atlantic Regional Educational Laboratory.

Leverett, L. (2011). The urban superintendents program leadership framework. In R. S. Peterkin, D. Jewell-Sherman, L. Kelley, & L. Boozer (Eds.), *Every child, every classroom, every day: School leaders who are making equity a reality* (pp. 1–15). San Francisco, CA: Jossey-Bass.

Little, J. W. (2007). Teachers' accounts of classroom experience as a resource for professional learning and instructional decision making. *Yearbook of the National Society for the Study of Education, 106*(1), 217–240.

López, G. R. (2003). The (racially neutral) politics of education: A critical race theory perspective. *Educational Administration Quarterly, 39*(1), 68–94.

Loveless, T. (2011). *The tracking wars: State reform meets school policy*. Washington, DC: Brookings Institution Press.

Marshall, C. (2004). Social justice challenges to educational administration: Introduction to a special issue. *Educational Administration Quarterly, 40*(1), 3–13.

Marshall, C., & Oliva, M. (Eds.). (2006). *Leadership for social justice: Making revolutions in education*. Boston, MA: Allyn & Bacon.

McDonald, J. P., Mohr, N., Dichter, A., & McDonald, E. C. (2013). *The Power of Protocols: An Educator's Guide to Better Practice* (3rd ed.). New York, NY: Teachers College Press.

McKenzie, K. B., & Scheurich, J. J. (2004). Equity traps: A useful construct for preparing principals to lead schools that are successful with racially diverse students. *Educational Administration Quarterly, 40*(5), 601–632.

McMahon, B. (2007). Educational administrators' conceptions of whiteness, anti-racism and social justice. *Journal of Educational Administration, 45*(6), 684–696.

Milner, H. R. (2012). But what is urban education? *Urban Education, 47*(3), 556–561.

National School Reform Faculty. (2014). Setting agreements activity. Retrieved from https://www.nsrfharmony.org/wp-content/uploads/2017/10/SettingAgreementsW-Examples_0.pdf

The New Jersey Coalition for Diverse and Inclusive Schools. (2019). Retrieved from https://www.inclusiveschoolsnj.org

New York Times. (2015). A conversation on race: A series of short films about identity in America. Retrieved from https://www.nytimes.com/interactive/projects/your-stories/conversations-on-race

Noguera, P. A. (2003). The trouble with Black boys: The role and influence of environmental and cultural factors on the academic performance of African American males. *Urban Education, 38*(4), 431–459.

O'Dea, C. (2016). Interactive map: Segregation continues to be NJ's state of the state. NJ Spotlight. Retrieved from http://www.njspotlight.com/stories/16/12/01/interactive-map-segregation-continues-to-be-nj-s-state-of-the-state/

Orfield, G., Ee, J., & Coughlan, R. (2017). *New Jersey's segregated schools: Trends and paths forward.* Civil Rights Project-Proyecto Derechos Civiles.

Ortiz, F. I., & Ortiz, D. J. (1995). How gender and ethnicity interact in the practice of educational administration: The case of Hispanic female superintendents. In R. Donmoyer, M. Imber, & J. Scheurich (Eds.), *The knowledge base in educational administration: Multiple perspectives* (pp. 158–173). Albany: State University of New York Press.

Parker, L., & Villalpando, O. (2007). A race(cialized) perspective on educational leadership: Critical race theory in educational administration. *Educational Administration Quarterly, 43*(5), 519–524.

Peterkin, R. S. (2011). Scaling up: The key to school improvement. In R. S. Peterkin, D. Jewell-Sherman, L. Kelley, & L. Boozer (Eds.), *Every child, every classroom, every day: School leaders who are making equity a reality* (pp. 204–209). San Francisco, CA: Jossey-Bass.

Peterson, K. (2002). The professional development of principals: Innovations and opportunities. *Educational Administration Quarterly, 38*(2), 213–232.

Pollack, T. M., & Zirkel, S. (2013). Negotiating the contested terrain of equity-focused change efforts in schools: Critical race theory as a leadership framework for creating more equitable schools. *The Urban Review, 45*(3), 290–310.

Reardon, S. F., & Galindo, C. (2009). The Hispanic-White achievement gap in math and reading in the elementary grades. *American Educational Research Journal, 46*(3), 853–891.

Roberts, J. E. (2012). *Instructional rounds in action.* Cambridge, MA: Harvard Education Press.

Roegman, R., Allen, D., & Hatch, T. (2017). The elusiveness of equity: Evolution of instructional rounds in a superintendents network. *American Journal of Education, 124*(1), 127–159.

Roegman, R., Hatch, T., Hill, K., & Kniewel, V. (2015). Relationships, instruction, understandings: One district's implementation of rounds. *Journal of Educational Administration, 53*(5).

Rusch, E. A., & Horsford, S. (2009). Changing hearts and minds: The quest for open talk about race in educational leadership. *International Journal of Educational Management, 23*(4), 302–313.

School Reform Initiative. (n.d.) Protocols. Retrieved from https://www.schoolreforminitiative.org/protocols/

Sentencing Project. (2017). Washington, DC. Retrieved from https://www.sentencingproject.org/

Shields, C. M. (2010). Transformative leadership: Working for equity in diverse contexts. *Educational Administration Quarterly, 46*(4), 558–589.

Singleton, G. E. (2014). *Courageous conversations about race: A field guide for achieving equity in schools* (2nd ed.). Thousand Oaks, CA: Corwin.

Singleton, G. E., & Linton, C. (2006). *A field guide for achieving equity in schools: Courageous conversations about race.* Thousand Oaks, CA: Corwin.

Skiba, R. J., Horner, R. H., Chung, C. G., Rausch, M. K., May, S. L., & Tobin, T. (2011). Race is not neutral: A national investigation of African American and Latino disproportionality in school discipline. *School Psychology Review, 40*(1), 85.

Skiba, R. J., Simmons, A. B., Ritter, S., Gibb, A. C., Rausch, M. K., Cuadrado, J., & Chung, C. G. (2008). Achieving equity in special education: History, status, and current challenges. *Exceptional Children, 74*(3), 264–288.

Skrla, L., McKenzie, K. B., & Scheurich, J. J. (Eds.). (2009). *Using equity audits to create equitable and excellent schools.* Thousand Oaks, CA: Corwin.

Smith, E. J., & Harper, S. R. (2015). *Disproportionate impact of K-12 school suspension and expulsion on Black students in southern states.* Philadelphia: University of Pennsylvania, Center for the Study of Race and Equity in Education

Sparks, D., & Hirsch, S. (2000). *Learning to lead, leading to learn.* National Staff Development Council, Oxford, OH.

Stevens, W. D., & Kahne, J (2006). *Professional communities and instructional improvement practices: A study of small high schools in Chicago.* Chicago, IL: Consortium on Chicago School Research, University of Chicago.

Stoll, L., & Louis, K.S. (2007). *Professional learning communities.* London: Open University Press.

Sue, D. W., Capodilupo, C. M., Torino, G. C., Bucceri, J. M., Holder, A., Nadal, K. L., & Esquilin, M. (2007). Racial microaggressions in everyday life: Implications for clinical practice. *American Psychologist, 62*(4), 271.

Sue, D. W., Lin, A. I., Torino, G. C., Capodilupo, C. M., & Rivera, D. P. (2009). Racial microaggressions and difficult dialogues on race in the classroom. *Cultural Diversity and Ethnic Minority Psychology, 15*(2), 183.

Tatum, B. D. (2007). *Can we talk about race?: And other conversations in an era of school resegregation.* Boston, MA: Beacon Press.

Theoharis, G. (2007). Social justice educational leaders and resistance: Toward a theory of social justice leadership. *Educational Administration Quarterly, 43*(2), 221–258.

Theoharis, G., & Brooks, J. S. (Eds.). (2012). *What every principal needs to know to create equitable and excellent schools.* New York, NY: Teachers College Press.

Turnbull, B. J., Riley, D. L., Arcaira, E. R., Anderson, L. M., & MacFarlane, J. R. (2013). *Six districts begin the principal pipeline initiative.* New York, NY: Wallace Foundation.

Valencia, R. R. (2010). *Dismantling contemporary deficit thinking: Educational thought and practice.* New York: Routledge.

Wingfield, A. H. (2007). The modern mammy and the angry Black man: African American professionals' experiences with gendered racism in the workplace. *Race, Gender & Class, 14*(1/2), 196–212.

Young, M. D., & Laible, J. (2000). White racism, antiracism, and school leadership preparation. *Journal of School Leadership, 10*(5), 374–415.

INDEX

Wonderings
  Developing Patterns and Wonderings Protocol,
    143–144
  framing, 46–47
  instructional rounds and, 19
  sample, 47

sharing, 47–48
vignette on developing, 59–61

Young, Jacqueline A., 19, 67, 114, 125

Zirkel, S., 4

A SAGE Publishing Company

Helping educators make the greatest impact

CORWIN HAS ONE MISSION: to enhance education through intentional professional learning.

We build long-term relationships with our authors, educators, clients, and associations who partner with us to develop and continuously improve the best evidence-based practices that establish and support lifelong learning.

INTERNATIONAL

Solutions YOU WANT | Experts YOU TRUST | Results YOU NEED

EVENTS >>> **INSTITUTES**

Corwin Institutes provide large regional events where educators collaborate with peers and learn from industry experts. Prepare to be recharged and motivated!

corwin.com/institutes

ON-SITE PD >>> **ON-SITE PROFESSIONAL LEARNING**

Corwin on-site PD is delivered through high-energy keynotes, practical workshops, and custom coaching services designed to support knowledge development and implementation.

corwin.com/pd

>>> **PROFESSIONAL DEVELOPMENT RESOURCE CENTER**

The PD Resource Center provides school and district PD facilitators with the tools and resources needed to deliver effective PD.

corwin.com/pdrc

ONLINE >>> **ADVANCE**

Designed for K–12 teachers, Advance offers a range of online learning options that can qualify for graduate-level credit and apply toward license renewal.

corwin.com/advance

Contact a PD Advisor at (800) 831-6640 or visit www.corwin.com for more information